Lucille
and
The XXX Road

Nathan

Follow your dreams

Jim Oliver

Lucille
and
The XXX Road

◆

Around The World Man & Motorcycle

*A Personal Dream of Daring Adventure Becomes
Reality During a Global Tour on Two Wheels
Including Post Communist Russia Home of "The
XXX Road"*

Jim Oliver

iUniverse, Inc.
New York Lincoln Shanghai

Lucille and The XXX Road
Around The World Man & Motorcycle

Copyright © 2007 by Jim Oliver

iUniverse books may be ordered through booksellers or by contacting:

iUniverse
2021 Pine Lake Road, Suite 100
Lincoln, NE 68512
www.iuniverse.com
1-800-Authors (1-800-288-4677)

The views expressed in this work are solely those of the author and do not necessarily reflect the views of the publisher, and the publisher hereby disclaims any responsibility for them.

ISBN-13: 978-0-595-41724-7 (pbk)
ISBN-13: 978-0-595-86063-0 (ebk)
ISBN-10: 0-595-41724-8 (pbk)
ISBN-10: 0-595-86063-X (ebk)

Printed in the United States of America

For Molly

Contents

Preface

Living life for over six decades can expose one to many sports. In the early years a tricycle is introduced to many of us, then maybe a game of kick-the-can, then a bicycle, softball, basketball, baseball, tennis, football, golf, and many other sports. The ultimate payoff is when one excels at a sport; the feeling of accomplishment is immense.

Some individuals are introduced to motorcycling somewhere along the way. Not everyone gets the opportunity though since the sport is considered very dangerous and family members often tend to discourage any activity on motorized two wheel machines. Undoubtedly, motorcycling is dangerous and can cause permanent or fatal injuries just as football, skydiving, scuba diving, down-hill skiing, bird hunting, and many other sports do on occasion.

For some of us, motorcycling is our favorite sport. Why, can be difficult to explain. The sport just seems to grow within us over time to an ever-increasing level. For myself I tire, over time, of other sports and I have to take a break from them periodically—but that is not the case with motorcycling. Riding through 49 states, Canada, Mexico, and literally around the world, has just increased my desire for more. Everyone needs a level of interest in *something* to the degree of my interest in motorcycling. It can provide a healthy solitary escape to *something*, ownership in *something*, and a high level of expertise in *something*. I realized long ago that I am very fortunate to have found my *something* at an early age and it "stuck". Good luck on finding your *something*.

Acknowledgments

Thanks to Shelly Myers and Jeff Friesen for their editing services along with the necessary constructive feedback.

Thanks to the Colby Writer's Club for encouraging my writing style.

Thank you to the numerous clubs and organizations that requested my oral presentations on the global motorcycle trip, and encouraged me to finish the book.

A belated thank you goes to my English teacher at Washburn University that raved about my term paper on *Mark Twain—the Riverboat Pilot* in 1964.

And thank you to my wife Molly, for reviewing the book, offering suggestions, enduring the hours alone as I was writing or riding, providing encouragement, and most of all, for giving me the freedom to develop.

1

Elementary Adventure

The rear wheel of the mammoth and overloaded BMW dual purpose motorcycle was sway dancing under me all morning due to the constant application of power from the engine and poor footing from the deep shoulder-to-shoulder large diameter rock on the road surface. Initially, it was rather frightening and stressful to ride under those conditions for even a hundred yards, let alone 110 continuous miles. But once "in the groove" it was discovered that a person could even begin to relax a little and enjoy the dance. But every now and then, my mind would drift into negative thoughts and enter the visualization of going down—in the rock—at 50 miles per hour, or more. Stupidity or denial sometimes overshadows the realization that it could happen to me. Reality tells me that going down in the rock would be a trip to the nearest hospital, get the hundred and some sutures, a cast, and some painkillers. Recovery would last a few weeks, or more. This would all occur just 12,000 miles from home in the desolation of East Siberia Russia.—From the Around the World journal, May 25, 2004.

What would make a person voluntarily subject himself to that kind of danger? That question has come up in my thoughts many times and the answer is always the same, "It is not real clear except for the love of the outdoors, 80 horses between my legs, living large, and the thrill of adventure".

My sense of adventure can be traced back to age three when preparation had begun for the ride of a lifetime, on a tricycle. The event took place in Topeka, Kansas; I lined up out in the middle of the street, at the top of a steep hill. On the really steep half of the block, the west half, rider and tricycle were ready to go for "the big thrill".

Growing up without a lot of parental boundaries, my learned behavior was to do what felt best. There was rarely anyone there to say, "Now Jimmy, have you given this a lot of thought"? There was no holding back.

Not being exactly sure what it was going to be like to go down that big hill just seemed to add to the excitement. One thing was certain, pedaling would be easy and that should be a real hoot. As it turned out, that was the understatement of the year—1946. As the ride commenced, the tricycle took off and gained speed as if it were pushed out of an airplane. Within a short distance the pedals were going around on that twenty-inch front wheel so fast that holding contact with the pedals was a futile effort. Controlling the forward speed and any thought of braking were not going to happen from then on. The hill was at least 75 yards long and I crossed the Mulvane Street intersection as if a high-speed police pursuit were in progress. Amazingly, I did not wreck and the tricycle eventually stopped; only then due to fright, did my breathing commence again. Living through that ordeal was a thrill permanently etched in my mind. That city block of Mulvane Street is gone now; the St Francis Hospital has taken it over for part of their mammoth complex. Thankfully, they are saving some other three-year-old from involuntarily filling his pants.

The ordeal with the tricycle was not all bad even though it was frightening at certain points of the trip. When I was flying down that hill on my tricycle I felt tremendously alive and in perfect balance. I now believe that in the innocence of my childhood I already possessed all that I truly needed to experience the joy that life offers. That feeling of being alive and in perfect balance with the world was with me then and has always been with me; I just forgot to believe in it.

I feel very sad that somewhere along the way, while growing up, the magic of make believe that lead to my dreams was forgotten and put aside. I also believe that the very first "three-wheeled" experience was never to be forgotten. It was tattooed upon my soul, waiting for the perfect moment to ignite the flame of passion to ride and be free.

During the first grade, my teacher, surely unintentionally, confused me on learning how to read and I developed a real disliking for the process. Consequently, from then on, reading was avoided by me whenever possible. Escape and evasion was practiced and perfected on reading until a later teacher, maybe during the 4th or 5th grade, noticed my tendency to avoid reading. The teacher kept insisting that I read a book and then hand in a book report. There was no argument from me but my intention was to do it in retirement when there would be more time available.

One day the teacher handed me a book and said, "here, read this and report on it"! Panic set in until I noticed the title, *Around the World in 80 Days*. Now that caught my attention. Could it be that one could actually enjoy reading a whole book? There was just enough curiosity that night as I opened the book that soon a process of putting the words to thought ensued. The process couldn't be stopped; there was an intellectual undertaking being fueled by the adrenaline of armchair adventure. Reading that book became more important than sleep or food. That was the first of many obsessive undertakings for me. The slow reading skills did not improve just because the subject matter was of high interest. In fact, the speed may have slowed down some due to the desire to absorb every letter of every word and every word of every paragraph. The magnetism to the adventure glued me to the book. Therefore, the book was completed in just a couple of days and the report was easy since the book was practically memorized and etched into my mind.

A dream was born. The dream would grow ever so slowly but life would always cultivate the dream. Someday, I too, would go around the world, but maybe not on a rickshaw, the back of an elephant, or in a hot air balloon. The thought of seeing the world was thrilling. I began thinking about:

- Seeing and meeting the quite different people of other countries

- Feeling the crazy weather other countries encounter

- Seeing the animals that inhabit other parts of the world

- Telling people of other countries about America

- Viewing the landscape in other sections of the world that is so different from Kansas

- The obsession to see the world—what a thrill that would be

Motorcycle careers don't begin by taking 40 mph curves at 80, or taking the solo trip up the infamous Dalton Highway of Alaska from Fairbanks to Prudhoe Bay, or the slow and nasty 80 miles south of San Felipe, Mexico. One works up to those events over a period of many years. More and more comfort can be gained over the years in greater and greater extreme riding by studying the sport, paying the dues, and practicing the necessary skills.

When thinking of discomfort, I am reminded of the day in 1980 when my wife Molly and I took a borrowed Honda 400cc motorcycle from Colby, Kansas to Norton, Kansas, round trip. That would be about 170 miles and it was very early in my motorcycle-touring career. The wind was blowing very strong out of the South, a common occurrence in Western Kansas. That presented a gusting crosswind for us as we trekked Northeast up highway US 83. Of course, we took some extra clothing with us, a picnic lunch, a camera and some other incidentals. So let's see, we were two-up on a rather small and under powered 400cc motorcycle, with extra gear strapped on, a heavy gusting crosswind, and the pilot-in-command, me, had little motorcycle-touring experience, let alone, experience with a passenger. Those circumstances would be a challenge for most riders—especially for someone with little touring experience. Whenever we stopped to get a soda pop or go to the bathroom we didn't talk much to each other. We were probably thinking the same thing, "I will be killed as a gust of wind blows us into a passing truck and everyone in the world will know how stupid I was—and it will hurt." God must take care of the ignorant since we survived that introductory venture.

Pretty soon, if a motorcyclist lives through the initial trials of perfecting motorcycle-riding skills, the motorcyclist becomes a veteran of the sport. Statistics show that most serious motorcycle accidents happen in the early stages of a motorcyclist's career (often in the first few hours) and the rider is usually within 30 miles of home. On a visit to the County Club Plaza in Kansas City, I was describing the Round the World Motorcycle trip to a sales clerk and she was quick to explain that her dad was killed on a motorcycle when she was six years old. He was simply taking the motorcycle around the block as a test drive while contemplating a purchase of the bike. He never made it around the block alive. What a tragic event that must have been for a young family to endure. It is my prayer that none of the readers of this publication become fatal motorcycle statistics.

My love for motorcycles can be traced back to a particular event. Until that summer motorcycles seemed too scary to consider as a sport. In the summer after my 6th grade our family moved back into the city of Topeka after having lived three years just beyond the city limits. Neil, another future 7th grader, and I, quickly became good friends. Neil had an older brother and the two of them owned a 125cc Harley Davidson Hummer. Now a Hummer to a 6th grader looked like a real "Hog", a big Harley. The Hummer was the most masculine machine ever witnessed by me, it was about my size, and it was love at first sight. My desire for ownership of a Hummer was huge. Neil would let me sit on the Hummer if I begged him and promised to be careful. After working on Neil for weeks to let me ride it, he finally conceded and said, "It's pretty hard to start—if you can get it started you can ride it." It was difficult to contain my enthusiasm over the prospect of riding that motorcycle and I felt all giddy inside—like I had just lost my virginity. Of course, the Hummer had a kick-starter. Even if it was in perfect tune one had to hold his mouth just right to get it started. Had that Harley been in gear while being kick started that summer, it would have gone across the state of Kansas and back, even though it never fired once.

The summer was over, it was time to go to the 7th grade, and it was time to quit kicking the Hummer. The little motorcycle never did start for me. I've never ridden a Hummer but it was that Harley Hummer Motorcycle that got my juices flowing. The thought of riding a motorized 2-wheel machine through the countryside, with the wind in my face, in total freedom, traveling very fast, in complete solitude, without the necessity of pedaling, sounded too good to be true. The obsession of becoming a motorcyclist was formed in my mind and would be kindled over time to become a lifelong sport. I had not yet put the two dreams together in my mind, going around the world and motorcycling.

2

Moped, Ducati, Yamaha &
Budweiser

After my right leg healed up from kicking the Harley Hummer all summer it was time to start working on mom to let me buy a Sears Roebuck Allstate Moped. Now the Moped was little more than a bicycle, at least that is what mom was told, but they would start and run and the GFA speed, Guts Feathers and All, was 42 mph.

After working on mom for months she was caught in a weak moment and we headed for Sears. Sears provided the financing for that new $162 Moped in 1956—thanks Sears for helping me get started on what was to become a lifelong sport. We signed all the papers, the salesman handed me the keys, and I proceeded to *push* it down the street until out of sight. It crossed my mind that hanging around too long would expose my total ignorance of the proper starting, riding and maintenance procedures of the machine. If this was discovered, someone like mom would change her mind about the purchase and the Moped would quickly become history. Once out of sight, the operator's manual could be pulled out and reviewed to determine how to start it, how to shift it, and how to fill it with gas. Since it wasn't much different than a bicycle to ride, the skill level rose rapidly on the Moped.

My first motorcycle accident occurred during the time that I owned the Moped but it was not on the Moped. A friend that owned a step-through Cushman Scooter had agreed to trade machines with me for the day. While showing off for some junior high girls and rounding a corner too fast, I steered through some sand in the intersection resulting in the Cushman and I sliding into a parked car. After practically taking off the left front fender of the car, peeling some sheet metal off the Cushman, and just about killing myself, I vowed to never show off on a motorcycle again, but I've cheated a few times. The Moped was good to me. I loved that little rascal. Unknowingly, I was slowly building the necessary skill on a method of transportation that would eventually carry me, and my gear, around the world.

More motorcycles were purchased over the years and it would be unkind to bore the reader with each war story but the sport grew stronger within me and tiring of the sport has never occurred. My first dirt bike was a 100cc Ducati Mountaineer. It was the coolest dirt bike you ever saw but it was a "little" hard to start. I owned it for about 3 months from January to March. Preparation for the typical ride on the Mountaineer that winter would include a couple of sweatshirts, long underwear, heavy coat, helmet, leather boots and some heavy gloves; then it was time to kick that Ducati to life. But it wouldn't start! After 45 minutes of kicking the starter the clothes were shed back down to my long handles—sweat was spewing profusely from my body. After it had been kicked enough, that the whole engine was warmed up, it would take off and run, but not necessarily for a long time. Next, the challenge was to work the throttle with one hand to keep it running while putting all my clothes back on. You can now see why it was only in my motorcycle stable three months. In the spring, the "Mountaineer" was traded for a brand new Yamaha 250cc DT-1 Enduro. That was one fun bike and I fell deeply in love with the sport as a result of the top performance of that medium sized Yamaha. It had much more capability than I had skill and that is the ratio between man's skill and machine's capability that I have desired ever since. On the bikes that I ride seriously, there is always more performance available from the bike whenever the situation calls for it. I simply have to take from the bike what I am capable of handling.

Many weekends were spent with my friends riding dirt bikes along the river and through abandoned rock quarries in the Topeka, Kansas area. Dirt biking is a wonderful sport in parts of the country where the terrain presents a challenge. Those were some of the most exciting recreational times of my life. I was also beginning to ride the DT-1 to work since it was so much fun.

I entered some Enduro competitions in my early motorcycle years. Enduros take the rider through some rugged conditions, such as up and down creek banks or across freshly plowed muddy fields, and the rider is to report into checkpoints along the route at specific times. The rider gets docked for points if he is too early or too late at the checkpoints. Enduros can put man and machine to great tests of endurance, of course.

My first Enduro race included great gobs (motorcycle technical term) of mud. My buddies and I rode together and helped each other through the really tough spots. We worked extremely hard on that competition and we reported in at the end of the race right on time, and we were first. We had won—we thought!

When the judge looked at our score card he said we missed 20 of the 60 miles. I thought that was close enough but the judge disagreed. We were so muddy that we had to ask for each other's name to communicate—we were unrecognizable.

Each motorcycle ride was better than the last one. Each motorcycle ride created a sense of adventure. There was no question in my mind that my heart was with motorcycling. It may be noteworthy that I started riding motorcycles before it was cool to ride a motorcycle! If I wasn't dreaming about going around the world, I was dreaming of motorcycles.

In my late twenties I was transferred to the High Plains of Colby, Kansas as a salesman. For those that have never experienced the High Plains, it is an area of flat terrain, very few trees, a scarcity of ground water, crops of corn, wheat, and sorghum, cattle feedlots, low humidity, and a light to heavy breeze on most days. Good country living and solid family values are still prevalent on the High Plains. The area however has a noticeable deficit of good dirt biking trails. Sandpits are scarce and rock quarries, as I knew them from Eastern Kansas, are essentially non existent.

My twenties also saw an increase in my alcohol consumption; it climbed to the excessive stage. The alcohol did not agree with my system either. My body reacted as though I was drinking poison and my thought processes became distorted and suspicious. I would begin a binge of drinking every night at 5:00 and the one-man party would go until about 2 AM. With the aid of alcohol I made a lot of poor choices, I developed many character defects, and my self esteem plummeted. My life consisted of working full time, going to night school part time to continue my college education, trying to help raise two boys, and at times utilizing a part time job to supplement the family income. That lifestyle did nothing to provide me with a feeling of serenity or contentment. It seemed to me that pouring more alcohol on the subject was the thing to do. Of course it is easy to see now that my life was too full and the burden too heavy for me to handle. But I do not use that situation as an excuse to drink. Finding time to drink was difficult but any good alcoholic can overcome that obstacle with just a little bit of ingenuity.

During my drinking career there were many car wrecks, more than I care to count. The first car wreck, when drunk, was at age 15. The last one was at age 32. That last one really was a tough one to get by the law without a DWI; back in those days it was called Driving While Intoxicated rather than Driving Under the Influence. But the Highway Patrolman turned his head once again as they did for most drunk drivers in those days. It was an absolutely horrible and terrifying night—a real nightmare by any standards. It scared me so much I didn't drink anymore—until the next night.

The disease of alcoholism, as the medical profession calls it, is cunning, baffling, and powerful. It had a death grip on me and it wouldn't turn loose but I couldn't see it. I was in denial, and no human being could penetrate my thinking. It seemed to me that a fifth of bourbon a day or a case of beer was ok and normal—I really believed that absurdity. After all, didn't everyone drink that way? The insanity had set in pretty deep for me.

My pain was intense from the emotional roller coaster of the drunkenness, hangovers, and constant battles at home—what was wrong with me? What a miserable life I was leading. I could not figure out the source of the problem—the denial was deeply entrenched. I was so disappointed in life and where life had taken me. Resentments and anger toward others set in and deep scarring within my family developed. I was spiritually, emotionally, financially, mentally, and physically bankrupt and the family was in trouble. I thought there was no reason to continue my life so I was contemplating ending it all.

Toward the end of my drinking career I found myself many times on my knees in a hotel room, after a night out on the town, praying to a God that I didn't even believe in to help me—I was desperate. My prayer was, "God, if you are out there, I need you to come into my life—I'll do anything to feel better." Sincere prayer works—at least it did for me! If one truly wants what he asks for in the prayer, and it does not conflict with what is in the bible, I believe God will listen.

The following is the most joyous story I could ever convey to you. Upon waking up one Sunday morning in January 1979, I realized before even getting out of bed, that something had happened overnight. I was a believer in God. It was an absolutely crazy feeling of giddiness. It was a wonderful feeling of comfort, joy, contentment, and togetherness with God. My age that morning was 35. I felt his presence and I knew I would not have to go through life ever again feeling as if I were alone. It was a gift from God and one of the greatest events of my life. I will cherish that born-again-experience forever. One can never adequately repay God for a gift such as I received that Sunday morning but it is sad to say that my drinking continued beyond that Sunday morning for another 13 months. I received many more obvious gifts from God, over the next few years, as I was still fighting the alcohol.

I hit bottom with my alcoholism when I discovered that I was having physical problems such as bleeding ulcers, psychological problems like wanting to die, marital problems as in divorce, and financial problems. I had a child-like spirit with God but I lacked the discipline to stay in the spirit since I was engulfed in problems. The divorce was a very painful experience for me especially since I was in such a weak psychological condition. Breaking up a family of four, along with all of those negative circumstances, really got my attention. I concluded, with the help of my higher power, whom I choose to call God, and a 12-step program, that I had to give up drinking forever. I didn't drink normally and, apparently, I never would be able to drink normally. If I drank, and could not control myself when I drank, I would always be a menace to society, family, future employers, the law, and myself. So, I had a revelation, another gift from God, that I was on a path of destruction with my drinking and I had to change.

I didn't want to be just another no-good bum. I didn't want to continue with my low-life ways. Something had to change if I was to ever find peace of mind and, what the 12-step program calls, serenity. Ah, serenity, could I ever find something as satisfying as contentment in me? I wanted to feel better and I would go to any length to get it. I was desperate and ready for a change.

I quit drinking on February 20, 1980 and God began to carry me because I did not have the strength or the fortitude to succeed. I attended the 12-Step meetings, I went to inpatient alcohol treatment and I found a little hope, which I hung onto with a death grip. With hard work over the years, and the grace of God, my life has turned around 180 degrees—quite literally.

I am very thankful that I did not drive a motorcycle when I had been drinking. I would not have survived. For 21 years, while I took time out to be a drunk, my dreams were put on hold.

3

Coast to Coast

My motorcycle career had also been put on hold since the high plains did not provide the type of dirt riding I preferred. I really struggled with not being able to get out in the country on weekends and do some hill climbing or play some "ditch-em" in the timber. I continued to read the motorcycle magazines and fantasized about the sport but I was out of the game for a few years. I just couldn't see myself riding a street bike and having any fun. After all, how much fun could it be to ride down a road with no obstacles to maneuver around? How boring that must be.

In pure desperation for the lack of a better plan, I purchased a brand new street bike in 1980. It was a sleek looking Honda CB900 Custom equipped with a heavy bulky Vetter Fairing and windshield on the front, Vetter saddle bags, a luggage rack, and a throttle lock. I was all set for some serious highway boredom. The CB 900 felt great from the saddle, it had adequate power, and it had a unique 10-speed transmission that was rarely seen on a street bike. My 900 ate engine oil. The dealer and I could never determine where the oil was going since the 900 didn't smoke out the exhaust or leak around the seals. I guess the oil just went to motorcycle heaven. It wasn't a serious problem but I carried extra engine oil and would add a quart every 800 miles if I rode fast and hard—which was always.

I put together what seemed like a monstrous trip—California and back in the spring of 1980. I was single at the time and I was giving myself a treat for staying sober a few months. I've made the trip by motorcycle many times since then; I thought of it back then on the same magnitude as going to the moon. The trip turned into quite an adventure. Ron Kaus, a fellow worker and I, took off after lunch one day in May in the rain. We rode to eastern Utah and camped out under the stars the first night and woke up the next morning staring at some beautiful red mountains. I was startled that morning by the magnificence. We experienced treacherous gusting crosswinds, heavy Southern California traffic, initiation into splitting the lanes, and the awesome Big Sur area up north. The challenge of San Francisco's steep grade intersections and riding in snow for hundreds of miles in freezing cold weather was almost too much for us. But the need to push to return home on time kept us moving forward. I can't speak for Ron, but I was hooked on motorcycle touring. That trip provided me adventure, lasting memories, and a deeper appreciation for the American Landscape.

Over the years I gravitated to other bikes, longer trips, and different destinations. One bike trade after another took me to more Honda, Yamaha, Harley, and BMW brands. They are all good but some bikes are better than others. I'm ashamed and proud at the same time, to say that I have no brand loyalty. I like the sound and the feel of a Harley, I like the performance of the BMW, and I love the brute power and reliability of the Japanese bikes. I just love the sport of motorcycling with a strong allegiance to no one manufacturer—just keep competing for our business guys!

It has often been said that motorcycle dealers could sell a lot more bikes if it weren't for wives and mothers. I lucked out when Molly picked me to be her husband. We started our relationship as great friends and that adds a dimension to a marriage that some people never experience. Molly is mentally strong and very intelligent, and always wants to please. We discovered somewhere along the way that best of friends want the best for each other. People don't want to suffocate their true friends. But it sure takes a lot of courage to let that friend spread their wings.

Molly has lost several family members to death over the years, starting with her mother at age 12. She was the oldest child still at home, and her dad, being a heavy drinker, was not available much of the time. Molly would not want to think of that situation in these terms, but rising to the occasion of rearing her sisters starting at age 12, made her a stronger person. That is a difficult way to gain strength but that is the hand she was dealt so she played it and made it work—for her, and her sisters. Because of Molly's strength and desire to let me be me, I was able to take several three-day to two-week solo motorcycle trips in the 1980's and 1990's. Molly's plate was full being a successful Realtor and raising her two children, my step-children.

One trip after another led me to major cities of 49 states in the United States, Canada, and Mexico. I've ridden 5th Avenue and Wall Street in New York City and the gorgeous Henry Hudson Parkway. I rode the "Dragon" on the Tennessee and North Carolina State lines—318 curves in 11 miles. I've zigzagged over the Rocky Mountains of Colorado numerous times. In 2003, I mastered the infamous Dalton Highway from Fairbanks to Prudhoe Bay, Alaska—solo. The heavy traffic of Boston rush hour and the notorious Sturgis Motorcycle Rally, 18 out of the last 19 years, were tackled. The Blue Ridge Parkway and scenic US 36 Highway across Kansas were special events. One of my favorite rides in the world is Independence Pass in Colorado. America is an amazing wonderland and my experiences of seeing her from the unobstructed view of two wheels are invaluable. I love you, America!

Still, I was dreaming of going around the world and it was becoming more important to me every day. I just did not know how I would do it, how I would afford it, or when I would attempt the expedition.

After all of those riding experiences the question became, "What would a guy do next—go around again"? That is not a bad thought. I noticed that when I took the same scenic road in the reverse direction it provided a completely different experience. The scenery seemed like I had taken a different road the second time through. Maybe that would provide a new challenge for me in my motorcycle career.

One year I attended an International Motorcycle Exposition in Denver. I stumbled onto an old dilapidated Harley Davidson Sportster on display and an awkward walking gentleman who struck up a conversation with me. His name was Dave Barr and he said that it was his motorcycle and he had ridden it around the world. Dave told me he was giving presentations on his RTW tour at the exposition and the next one was in just a few minutes. RTW is motorcycle lingo for Round the World. I went in and sat down right up-front. For the next hour I let Dave mesmerize me with pictures and narration of his adventures while riding the Harley around the world for 83,000 miles. His struggles were numerous and his stamina and determination to succeed were put to an hourly test—day after day.

Dave's accomplishment in riding a motorcycle around the world was spectacular even more so, at least in my mind, since Dave has no legs—only prosthesis.

Dave Barr lost his legs in a mercenary accident in Africa. Dave told the story about how he was lying around his home in California after the accident feeling sorry for himself when his mother said, "Dave, you have to get up and go make something of yourself". Dave decided to ride around the world on a motorcycle. What an inspiration he has been for us long distance riders who have all of our limbs. His book, *Riding the Edge* tells how he fell down over and over, had a tough time getting the bike upright and himself back in the saddle, only to go a few yards before falling down again. I have told myself over and over, "If Dave Barr can go RTW with no legs I ought to be able to do it with both of my legs in tact".

A long, long time ago, maybe 20 years, my wife Molly and I were struggling with everything from finances to religion and we were arguing most of the time. One weekend we took off for Denver, rented a nice hotel room, and spent most of the weekend in that room discussing what we wanted to accomplish as individuals and as a couple. We looked at our careers, finances, church, family, recreation, and our health. At the close of the weekend we had developed a list of specific written goals that had a date attached to each one of them—and we owned the goals. Some of the goals had a time line as long as five years away. As a result of that weekend, two things happened. First, we came home with a huge load lifted from each of us and we had a new lease on life. We knew what we were going to work on next and what our spouse had planned to accomplish. Secondly, we hit each goal and we hit them right on time. The outcome was amazing and that exercise instilled in me that <u>written</u> goals get accomplished. A few years after that exercise I became a financial planner. I had no trouble buying into the concept of identifying, prioritizing and writing down one's goals—unless, of course, you do not care where you end up.

A story about a POW comes to mind when I think about goal setting. It is important to be able to visualize the attainment of the goal. The story goes like this; a POW, who had never played a game of golf, spent a great deal of time visualizing every finite detail of the golf swing. He was doing this as a diversion, of course, for his mind to help him get through the horror of the day. By visualizing every detail of the golf game he was eventually released from captivity as a respectable golfer at the outset. He just knew how to do it because he had "seen it" in his mind.

Somewhere along the way I resurrected that old idea of going around the world and I began thinking about using two wheels to carry my gear and me. I wanted to accomplish something just for me and I did not care whether I impressed anyone else with my adventure. I had fallen in love with the motorcycle sport and I wanted to leave something behind for the next rider—kind of a legacy.

During one of my personal and business planning sessions in 1998 I wrote down a goal. The goal was; *"I will go solo around the world on a motorcycle by my age 60"*. Now let me clarify; I had no idea how that was going to happen, but I was quite sure if I was not willing to write it down, it had no chance of accomplishment. The word "solo" was important in the written goal since that told me that if no one else wanted to join me, I would go it alone. The planning that began immediately on the project was rather amazing. I had started the clock on a goal just five years away; there was a lot to consider, so I decided I had better get started. I was buying into the dream—the trip of a lifetime.

I struggled with the idea of going around the world since I had a wife and a financial planning practice full of great clients here at home that I cared about very deeply. I have the greatest wife a motorcyclist could ask for but she was really having trouble with this trip. I prayed to God often that he would show me the way. "If I am on the wrong track please show me where I am wrong God". I watched very closely for signals that he sometimes sends my way. Every time I met an obstacle in the planning of the trip, it would be miraculously resolved and another little smile would crop up on my face.

In the year 2002, about two years before the trip, I split the goal into two parts. The goals would be (*1*) *Go around the world on a motorcycle by age 60 and* (*2*) *Do it quickly.* I discovered that the desire to accomplish the goals was so intense that I was willing to die trying to achieve those goals. Not that I would die, but it was that intense. I could "see" myself accomplishing the RTW tour. I committed to those two goals and, in the year 2002, I set a departure time of May 15, 2004 at 2 PM (we actually flew out of Denver 7 ½ hours later at 9:30 PM on May 15, 2004 to meet the bikes in Vladivostok, Russia). The planning intensified at that "commitment date" and the juices began flowing. My dream was coming true. Hot damn, I'm going around the world!

4

Plan—Plan—Plan

How do you eat an elephant—one bite at a time. I really did not see the RTW tour as an elephant size task. It would just be another long distance tour and I would break it down into several daily rides. Admittedly, it did present some real challenges in the planning:

- How would I keep the tigers from eating me?

- How would I ship the bike across two oceans?

- What if I get sick or have an accident overseas?

- How do I stay in contact with home while in Siberia?

- How would my clients deal with me being gone for two months?

- Can I handle the solitude?

- What motorcycle would work best?

- What if I ruin a tire in Siberia where new tires are scarce or non-existent?

- How do I converse with people speaking other languages?

- And the list goes on.

The planning was just as large of a task as imagined—or maybe even larger. As often as I could, I would chase down the answers to my questions either on the web, by email or with phone calls. I started two large 3-ring notebooks to keep track of things. Each contained several tabs: route, personal & family, bike & equipment, documents, gear, health, e-mail copies, business, communications and sponsors. The notebooks started filling up very fast and were soon bulging.

A time line of events was worked up on the computer. Each time I thought of an item that would need to be accomplished I would put it on the list in the proper order—according to the date it would need to be completed.

The most difficult task in planning was the shipment of the bikes across the Pacific Ocean. I wanted to ship by air but no airline wanted to fly the bikes into Russia. The Russians considered the motorcycles dangerous goods since they included gas tanks and electrical batteries. STS Logistics, in Tacoma, Washington was finally located and they did a marvelous job in shipping the bikes by sea.

Several months before take off I concluded that Molly might be a little more comfortable if I took someone with me on the trip. Dennis O'Neil, a good riding friend from Colorado, had ridden to Mexico with me and I had ridden to Alaska with him. I approached Dennis about going along with me on the RTW tour. Dennis is a retired engineer, has been a great student of motorcycling for about five years, and we had tested our tolerance for each other out in the "wild". Dennis began immediately in helping me plan the trip and he eventually decided he would join me on the journey around the globe.

The Internet is an amazing tool for research and communication. Long distance motorcyclists, especially RTW riders, have a pretty good communication system worldwide. Berndt Tesch of Germany told Frederic Journou, a Frenchman living in Los Angeles, that he should contact Jim Oliver in Kansas since both of us were going around the world on a motorcycle. Frederic emailed me and sure enough, he and I were going around the world about the same time, in the same direction and, at least initially, taking the same route. We began combining the results of our planning and decided we would try and ship our bikes together across the Pacific to save a few dollars. We had many email conversations and some telephone conversations for over a year but never met in person.

THE ROUTE—I would leave Colby, Kansas and ride to Seattle, ship the bike to Vladivostok, Russia and ride across all of Russia. I had a strong desire to see Siberia. I wanted to see first hand what was described to me over the years as a God-forsaken area of extremes—cold, poverty, and isolation to name a few. China would intentionally be avoided due to hassles of getting in and out of the country. After Russia, and entering Latvia, I would work my way southwest through Western Europe, ultimately riding the Dolomite Mountains of Italy, the Alps of Switzerland and France, and the Pyrenees Mountains of Spain. I would ship from the west coast of Europe back to the United States or Canada, hopefully, by air.

Due to the language barrier that I would encounter in Russia, I selected a route traveling east to west, as opposed to west to east. I believed it might be easier to get a motorcycle out of customs-arrival in Russia than on a ship in Russia with the hopes of it getting to the proper destination in the United States. In addition, an east to west route would give me a 25-hour day about every other day by turning the clock back as opposed to turning it ahead by going the other way. I later discovered that the longer days only contributed to the fatigue since I used the extra hour for riding rather than resting.

PERSONAL & FAMILY DETAILS—It seems like I have needed to lose a few pounds (okay a lot of pounds) all of my adult life. But this time I had more motivation to lose the excess baggage. I felt like I needed to get leaner and meaner to survive this trip. I wanted to be faster on my feet, stronger in my arms and legs, have more stamina, and have more confidence in taking care of myself. Who knew what I was getting into? I would lose 30 pounds, which would take me to 180 pounds. I made it to 188 lbs. at disembarkation day. For strength and stamina I purchased dumbbells and used them four times per week, and I walked many miles each week. I was in pretty good shape as I began the trip.

The County Health Nurse suggested I get Hepatitis and Tetanus shots and take one Malaria pill per week from one week before to three weeks after the trip. The nurse gave me the shots and my pharmacist had to order the malaria pills. My medical doctor gave me the go-ahead on the trip and he gave me several prescriptions for pills that I might need in a pinch while in remote areas of the world. I filled the prescriptions and carried them all the way around the world. Luckily, I didn't need Doc's pills but he said keep them—"they make a good travel kit wherever you go". I'm fortunate that I don't take pills regularly and I rarely need the services of a doctor.

In 47 years of on and off riding of motorcycles I have never needed medical attention for a motorcycle accident—but what if it happens for the first time in Siberia? I purchased a pre-paid medical evacuation plan that would send a jet aircraft after me if I were in a hospital and over 150 miles from home. The jet would then take me to the hospital of my choice, anywhere in the world, and I would choose the United States. The plan gave me great comfort in case of an accident or ill health. The plan covered one year for about $225. Anyone can purchase the plan from Air Med Traveler at 1-800-356-2161. In addition to hauling me around, Air Med said they would pick up Molly and bring her to the foreign country also.

Even though it seemed that I had lost my mind and was going into never-never land, Molly still needed to be able to function without me back home in case something went dramatically wrong. To solve that problem I gave her a Durable Power of Attorney for Business Reasons, a Durable Power of Attorney for Health Care Decisions, and my Living Will. With those documents Molly could buy or sell anything for us and she could make medical decisions for me if necessary. Once back home, I could simply take back the Durable Power of Attorney for Business Reasons since I could make those decisions for myself again. Those documents are not expensive through a competent attorney.

THE BIKE and EQUIPMENT—I chose to ride a BMW R1150GS due to its reliability, ease of maintenance, added safety features, and performance. I felt like I was going to get very close to this bike on an around the world tour. I was dependent on her to never let me down and she was dependent on me to pick a great route. I wanted to name her and I contemplated many names before I settled on "Lucille"—my wife's deceased mother's name whom I never had the pleasure of meeting. "Lucille" is painted on each side of the gas tank. I love you—Lucille.

Equipment on the bike amounted to extra lighting for night riding which was provided by Cycle Gadgets, an engine guard, the standard windshield, and a handlebar mounted GPS. The Adventure tank was installed for extra gas capacity, a tank bag for quickly needed small items, and a Bill Mayer custom seat that proved to be invaluable. Jesse hard panniers, a large capacity luggage rack, and Helen-2-Wheels soft bags were also used on the bike. I would start out with Metzler Tourance tires. Then I would change to the Metzler Karoo tires, "knobbies", at Tacoma, Washington, for the Siberian ride. I would strap on two new Metzler Tourance tires, on top of everything else, at Tacoma, to put on after the Siberian struggle. I used synthetic oils in all of Lucille's drive line compartments. It seems to me that everything works a little smoother with synthetics.

NECESSARY DOCUMENTS—Of course, one begins a trip such as this by dusting off his passport or buying a new one. Russia was the only country along the entire route that required a visa. I fretted over obtaining a Russian visa since one must be sponsored into the country and one cannot stay a single day past the visa expiration. I was led to believe that the 90-day business visa was very hard to obtain and I really wanted more than a 30 day visa since I estimated it would take 25 days to get across Russia and 5 days is not enough margin for error. As it turned out, one can obtain a 90-day visa to Russia over the Internet in about 2 weeks for $225 (www.gotorussia.com).

An International Driver's Permit was obtained and was invaluable. The IDP translates one's driver's license into about 10 different languages; you can just pick the languages you desire. The IDP can be obtained in a week or so through AAA for about $10; but make sure AAA puts your motorcycle endorsement on the IDP.

Since I was riding a motorcycle I had to carry my original title, my motorcycle registration, and my insurance card. Special liability insurance, just for Russia, had to be purchased as soon as I arrived in Russia. That was not extremely difficult to accomplish and I paid $33 for 30 days. Once I got through Russia, I bought liability insurance in Latvia for all of Western Europe for about $35 for another 30 days.

I needed a certified copy of my birth certificate and passport pictures in case I lost my passport. Heaven forbid if I had to present all of these documents to Russian officials. They would not be able to read them and I would not be able to interpret the documents for them.

Russian web sites suggested that I obtain a certificate from the Russian Government specifically authorizing me to bring a GPS and a Satellite Telephone into their country. I tried diligently to get the certificate but was unsuccessful. I wrote and called embassies, consulates, and the Russian Government in Moscow and Vladivostok, to no avail. I went anyway planning to ask forgiveness if apprehended; I do not recommend that you follow all of my ways. The Russians have been known to be paranoid about lots of things that we westerners take for granted. I had read that using a GPS in the wrong manner in Russia, such as doing mapping, could result in 10 years in jail. That would really throw me off schedule. It appears that the Russians are relaxing more and more every day as they see communism further in the distant past.

THE GEAR—Traveling light is imperative on a trip of this size. Lay out everything you think you will need and then put half of it back in the closet, seriously. I took 3 pairs of cotton cargo pants, 3 shirts, one fleece jacket, 3 sets of underwear, 3 sets of socks, a pair of walking shorts, a swimming suit which I never wore, some shower thongs, and some tennis shoes. Toiletries, a small towel, bar soap, a wind and rain hat, and a first aid kit were also packed. Tire changing tools, a hand-held air compressor, tire-plugging equipment, extra engine oil, necessary tools for the bike, and a motorcycle journal were all deemed necessary items. On top of all that I carried two new tires across Siberia.

I camped so I needed a durable small tent and footprint, an insulated mattress, a sleeping bag, and something for a pillow. A collapsible bucket is handy to have along and does not take much space.

Aerostich Motorcycle Clothing agreed to sponsor my trip. I wore their Darien Jacket and Darien Pants that were waterproof and windproof and offered built-in armor in the event of an accident. The Aerostich garments are a 10 in my book. I wore them everyday for the 60 days out on the road and I have no complaints of the Darien outfit. Just before the trip commenced, I replaced my old helmet with the new model. A full-face helmet is the only way to go for distance riding. I did not like the new Shoei helmet. It had too many air holes that had to be duct taped shut for warmth and the flip-up front did not want to release to flip up—once up, it wouldn't stay up. I took summer type Deerskin gloves (bought at the farm store) and winter type Gore-Tex gloves. I wore BMW waterproof boots and they really kept my feet warm and dry. I also threw in some thermal long johns just in case and an electric vest. I wore both the long johns and the electric vest throughout Siberia.

TAKING CARE OF BUSINESS—Preparing my business for an extended absence was added stress that some individuals would not have to contend with before leaving. In my case, I made sure my financial advisory clients new I was leaving and when I planned to be back. I met with each of them that wanted to, for client review sessions, within 90 days of the trip.

COMMUNICATIONS WITH AMERICA—A satellite telephone was carried around the world and I must say it worked quite well even in the bottom of a rock quarry in Siberia. Being in some contact with those back home was important to me. In my other life, I have a weekly radio broadcast on financial services which gives me some comfort in being on the airwaves. So I called a progress report into the local radio station with the satellite phone everyday and that was a huge hit with the public. People altered their schedules to make sure they could listen to the "crazies" going around the world. Youngsters, and oldsters, were encouraged to follow the adventure on a map or a globe. It proved to be a very good geography project back home. The daily updates also gave my wife a briefing on my progress and my health. There were a couple of times that I missed my opportunity to call in and that caused a big stir back home. Thousands of people followed my progress and lived my dream of going around the world via the radio. The satellite telephone was rented for $180 per month and $1.80 per minute for usage. The local telephone-company, S&T Communications sponsored the telephone rental and KLOE/KKCI radio, Goodland, Kansas provided the airtime.

SPONSORS—There is some debate as to whether sponsors are worth getting. Naturally, they want to be a part of the adventure, get some good advertising out of the event, but they do not want a big expense. At least a few sponsors are nice to have and some new relationships develop during the process.

5

Extreme Danger

As we got closer and closer to "jump off" day I became more nervous about taking on something of this size with a partner. Dennis was retired and I was still working. Dennis was living alone and I was married. With that said I felt like Dennis had much more flexibility with his time than I did, and that might cause a problem for us down the road. Dennis and I would meet for a couple of hours each month, before the BMW Motorcycle Club of Colorado meeting in Denver, for planning purposes. A couple of months before the trip began I wrote Dennis a letter and handed it to him at one of our planning sessions. I wanted him to know exactly what my expectations were of the trip and what my intended time schedule would be. I wanted him to be able to ask me questions and I wanted to know how my schedule was going to fit his desires. After reading the letter Dennis said, "Jim, I'll just follow you!" Dennis is a good leader in everything he does but this time he was just going to follow me around the world. That may have been the greatest compliment anyone ever gave me.

It was important to me to get through Siberia between the winter snows and the summer bugs. That would be the end of May or early June. It was agreed among Dennis, Frederic and me that we would all arrive in Vladivostok, Russia on May 17. Working backwards on the calendar regarding the shipment of the motorcycles it was determined that Dennis and I would need to leave Denver on April 9 to ride the distance to Tacoma, Washington, get the bikes serviced and tires changed, and have the bikes at the shipper on time. Our freight forwarder, STS Logistics said it would take about 3 weeks to ship the bikes over the Pacific to Vladivostok and they needed the bikes three days early to satisfy the U.S. Customs Department. The three of us agreed to meet at STS in Seattle on April 17.

April 8, 2004 was the day I left Colby, Kansas to begin the first of two legs on an around the world motorcycle tour. As the day approached the clock began spinning. Time was getting away from me. I thought I would never be ready and then I had a revelation—I could continue the planning of a trip of this sort for the rest of my life since so much of it was foreign to me. I had done an excellent job of planning and I would just go when the time came.

Molly and I did not talk much about the date—April 8. If we did not talk about it maybe this year we would just skip the 8th. Molly was concerned about my safety and her solitude. She handled herself much better than I could in her situation. She did not know how far I was willing to go trying to accomplish my dream, but she must have suspected my dedication because I was not nervous and I was quite focused. On the other hand, I had no intentions of dying on this trip because I could visualize every detail of the trip including the finish of riding back into Colby from the east when I had departed to the west. I suspect the Wright Brothers had no fear of flying back in 1903 even though no man had ever flown before. They could visualize flight, and they knew they would succeed. Their confidence overshadowed every negative thought that entered their minds. They never deterred from moving toward man's first flight.

April 8, 2004 arrived one day, just as the calendar had predicted. I always said I was going around the world just for me and not to impress anyone. It is a good thing! At 2 PM, the scheduled departure time, I put on my riding gear and loaded the bike. I jumped on Lucille, waved to the crowd (actually there was not one person standing there) and took off—toward Denver to the west.

It really was not a bad day to ride. The temperature was in the high 40s and there was a light rain. With the proper gear those are dandy conditions for long distance motorcyclists.

I arrived in Denver on time and went directly to the BMW of Denver motor-cycle dealer for their unveiling party for the R1200GS, the replacement model for Lucille. Dennis came to the shindig also and we had some last minute conver-sation about the trip and agreed to meet in the morning at 6:30 at Johnson's Cor-ner way north of Denver. Loaded and ready to ride, we would have some breakfast at Johnson's Corner, and head north.

The next morning I was up about 4:30 which is typical for me on a long ride. I rode in rain and middle 30s temperature up to Johnson's Corner. I ate so much for breakfast I thought I would have to put more air in my tires to carry the extra load; after all, I was on vacation! The waitress brought me eggs, hash brown pota-toes, sausage, biscuits and gravy, toast, and coffee. After that she said, "You ready for one of our cinnamon rolls"? I said, "Well, I guess so". Remember, I had been dieting and I had just escaped from that horrible treatment. Now the cinnamon roll was the type you would serve POW's in celebration of their release from 10 years of captivity—8" across, 3" deep, and floating in that sticky stuff that makes my teeth act all sexy. It was fabulously wonderful.

So after breakfast and lunch—all at one setting—it was time to ride. We headed north on Interstate 25 in the rain that was mixed with snow flurries. By the time we got to Cheyenne, Wyoming, just about 60 miles, I thought it would be a good idea to stop at the truck stop and check the road reports going west since the rain was now gone and we were only left with snow—heavy snow. All of the truckers were shutting down due to the winter weather conditions of snow and slush on the roadways. They were just going to wait out the storm. We concluded that they were real smart for being on the safe side but our motorcycles shouldn't have any trouble so off we went to the west on Interstate 80. The perceptive reader is now beginning to see patterns of insane behavior in Dennis and me. Actually, we rode pretty well that day except for the cold and we got a room at Little America, Wyoming, that night.

The next morning there was considerable snow on the ground and the parking lot of the motel had black ice—the worst nightmare of a motorcycle tourist. The temperature was slightly below freezing. We loaded the bikes and had a slow leisure breakfast to let the sun get up pretty high to melt the pavement. Dennis was watching the ice pretty closely and he was itching to ride. About 9 seconds after the ice had melted in the parking lot Dennis convinced me that we could go. Who was I to act cowardly? We headed out to the interstate highway riding kind of gingerly to get the feel of the road and headed up the on ramp to the Interstate with me leading. At the end of the on ramp I knew we were in big, dangerous, trouble. You see, the Interstate was covered with 6 inches of slush except for two tire tracks in the outside lane and the traffic was heavy since all of the truckers from Cheyenne were now rolling again—in a bunch, and the bunch was upon us. The words that I was saying under that helmet can never be repeated in modern civilization. My first thought was to pull over to the side so Dennis and I could talk about the situation. Then I quickly realized that I could not pull out of my track and into the slush or I would go down for sure and very possibly get run over by some of the heavy traffic. I could not stop since the traffic was heavy; in fact, the traffic was pushing us to go faster. Dennis and I had no communication between the bikes, which was a mistake, and the only thing to do would be to keep going. By this time my fears were numerous. Two of the immediate fears were the possibility of the track I was in turning to black ice or the track disappearing all together and the entire road surface turning to slush.

I'm not a betting man and I don't even buy lottery tickets, but I would have wagered a thousand dollars that morning that either Dennis or I would go down on the interstate. I would have bet you five hundred dollars that we would both go down. Had that happened we would have slid for a hundred miles, almost, while the truckers were using us for improved traction.

The truckers were having fun with us that nasty morning. I can't blame them either. Here you have two loonies on motorcycles trying to ride a high speed interstate highway in winter driving conditions and they are riding like they are scared to death. The truckers must have been thinking why not give them a hand and put them out of their misery? The truckers could handle the passing lane quite well since slush is not a major concern for them at 45 to 50 miles per hour—but we were going 25 to 35 miles per hour in the outside lane. As the trucks passed us they would throw a tidal wave of slush clear over our heads with each axle that passed. We would take our left hand, one of the two hands with the death grip on the handlebars, and make one quick swipe across our face shields and back to the handlebar. We still could not see but it made us feel better to wipe our face shields. That exercise would be repeated for every truck axle that went by us. I would hear a semi truck coming up on my left side and I would wonder, "Oh dear God, what have I done to make you so mad"? We rode that way for over and hour and a half and neither of us went down. "Thank you God, and forgive me for ever doubting your power"! In all of my motorcycle travels, that morning provided some of the most frightening miles ever experienced and we were just on day two of an around the world motorcycle trip.

Soon we were closing in on Salt Lake, the highway had cleared up, and we were running over 90 mph to make up for some lost time. When we finally stopped for lunch I don't think we even talked about the death-defying event—it was like it didn't happen. We did run into a trucker at the truck stop northwest of Salt Lake that saw us in Little America. He passed us out on the road, and was real impressed that we were still alive. Sometimes when I ride through this world, I am delighted to say, "Yes that was me that survived that ordeal". But that morning I was real embarrassed for people to know that I allowed myself to get into that situation. It was a terribly dangerous mistake that even a fool would not do—God had to carry us through it. Again, thank you God. The rest of the trip to Seattle and Tacoma was just plain vanilla. Nothing fancy, just a great ride in good conditions.

Dennis and I spent Easter dinner with his sister and family in Portland, Oregon. It gave us an opportunity to answer some more questions for the public about our adventure that was just beginning.

I took off by myself from Portland and left Dennis with his family. We met two days later at the BMW dealership in Tacoma to have last minute service done and change all the tires to get ready for Siberia.

We ran into Frederic for the first time the next day at Bremerton, Washington so we were ready to hand over all three bikes to STS Logistics. It was almost tearful for me to let Lucille go to Russia without me. What if she needed me? She would be so defenseless. Sometimes, we just have to be strong as we go through life.

After a leisurely lunch, Dennis and I parted ways once again with Frederic and we agreed to meet in Vladivostok, Russia (Vladi) on May 17. We all flew home, Dennis and I back to Denver, and Frederic back to Los Angeles. I would work in my business back in Colby for three more weeks before leaving on the larger second and final leg of the trip.

6

Flying to Siberia

Everything that could be left on the bikes was left on the bikes. We were just taking a chance that it would be okay since it would be impossible for us to carry all of that on the flight back home and then on another flight to Vladi. We left tents, sleeping bags, clothing, tools, first aid kits, and replacement tires on the bikes. STS said the bikes would go into a secured sea container and locked until we unlocked them in Russia—yea, yea, you can sure bet your life on that. We didn't have much choice since we could not physically carry all of that gear on our flights back home and then overseas.

The three weeks back home went by very fast and some people were wondering why I was home so quick—some thought I just went around the world real fast—in about a week.

I wanted to leave Molly with some written thoughts I had about our life and our marriage so I stopped one day and wrote her an eleven-page letter. It took me an hour and a half. I presented the sealed letter to her a few days before departure and she chose to open it after I got on the airplane. Molly and I went to Denver on May 14, spent the night with our kids and grandkids and we enjoyed a real fun surprise party that night for me, complete with a decorated cake.

The family had very little to do on the 15th except take me to the airport about 7:00 PM for my international flight to Russia departing at 9:30 PM. The closer we got to 7 PM the more anxious I got since it seemed that everyone else was anxious and no one knew quite what to say anymore. None of us knew exactly what I was getting into or just how much trouble I would encounter.

We had to decide who would take me to the airport and drop me off at passenger check-in. My son-in-law, my two grandsons, a nephew, and Molly and I jumped into the family van for the 20-minute ride to Denver International Airport. I had to be very careful at the airport to hold back the tears. It felt like I was saying goodbye to the family and going to war—what a selfish, self-centered thing I was doing! I felt a lot better though when my 4 ½ year old grandson

Noah, said, "Grandpa, you won't be scared or lonely because you have God with you". I thought about those words all the way around the world and how proud I was to be his grandpa.

Check-in and security were a piece of cake that night and when I got to the gate there was Dennis, right on time. We had a pleasant flight to Los Angeles, a short lay—over and then an international flight on Asiana Air to Inchon, Korea. The flight over the Pacific took 13 hours. It was dark for the entire flight since we were chasing the sun and took off from LA at midnight. Even at that, the hostesses were bringing us food or drink about every half-hour and checking on our well being. There is a lot of difference in the service between an international flight and a domestic flight. We lost the day of May 16th by flying over the international dateline. I would get that day back one hour at a time by traveling through the time zones around the world.

At the Inchon airport we had our first experience on the trip with currency exchange. We paid for our coffee and roll with U.S. dollars and received change in Won. I had no idea what happened since I did not know what the exchange rate was at the time.

Inchon has one of the cleanest and prettiest airline terminals that I have seen but it still does not feel like home—there were Koreans everywhere. We had about three hours in Inchon before our short flight on Korean Air up to Vladivostok. Frederic was on that flight so we three had been brought together once again.

Landing at Vladivostok was a different experience. The runway was just cut out of a forest with no terminal in sight upon landing. It seemed like we taxied for an hour and after rounding one corner, "shazam", there was a terminal. I am accustomed to the pilot pulling up real close so I can just walk through a corridor to the main terminal. But at Vladi they just shut her off out on the tarmac and pull up a portable set of stairs to the side of the bird. The experience of disembarking from that airplane set the stage for the next four days. There were about 15 Russians, of different uniforms, lingering around our "stairway to Russia" but no one was talking—not at all. They had grim expressions for us visitors. Some had drawn guns at the ready position. One of them motioned for us to get on the waiting buses, which we all did without question, but I sure wondered where they were going to take us. Literally, they drove us 30 yards and we all got off and filed into the terminal. There were three long lines inside and the three of us bikers picked one, not knowing what we were doing. At the front of the line, was a pretty young Russian lady sitting a little higher than eye-level, behind bulletproof glass, to look at the immigration documents we were carrying. There was a small tray in the bottom of the glass front of her secured small office to slide documents back and forth. What I found real interesting though was the door to her little room, within arms length of me, was propped wide open for ventilation. Next, we went to another window where the attendant checked our passport, visa, and the previously issued immigration certificate again. Just around the corner, all of the plane's bags had gone through x-ray and ours were ready to be picked up. We were out of there pretty quickly and into the common area where people were waiting to welcome passengers, but not us. I could breathe a little easier now that I was through customs since I was carrying a GPS and a satellite telephone, and I had no Russian Government authorization to carry them. I say a little easier, I still had to sweat being caught with the two items every time I was stopped in Russia by the authorities.

Dennis and I were concerned that we had not declared to anyone that we were attached to another shipment, namely our bikes. We had read many times that we needed to make our declaration at customs. A representative with the U.S. Embassy happened to be there picking up a document and, after checking with Russian Customs Authorities, he told us we did not need to declare. That was very bad advice that would haunt us over the next four days. Again, RTW motor-cycle riders have a pretty good communication system via the Internet. Dennis and I were to meet Igor "Sinus", a resident of Vladivostok, soon after arrival and he would help us with the details of getting our bikes out of customs. I somehow came in contact years ago with Sinus over the Internet. When he went through the United States in 2002 I was available to put him up in a motel room and buy him a couple of meals—which was the least I could do for a fellow RTW biker. While I was busy with other duties at the terminal Dennis was able to contact Sinus by phone and let him know that we had arrived. Sinus, a TV journalist in Vladivostok, was busy at the moment and he said to just give him a call when we got downtown. No problem but, "where is downtown, we thought"? How do we negotiate with these cunning looking taxi-drivers that talk Russian? How do we know we are getting an acceptable deal on the taxi ride? Where do we get let off in this city of a million people? Where do we tell Frederic we will be? How do we contact him again so we can get our bikes out of customs together?

Frederic had another Igor lined up to meet him at the airport to help him with the details of being in a foreign city with a huge language barrier, and no idea of how to proceed with anything. In the front lobby of the terminal, Dennis, Frederic, and I were trying to work out the logistics of how we proceed. Eventually, Frederic asked his Igor if he would mind giving Dennis and I a ride downtown. What was Igor going to say? He agreed so Dennis and I grabbed all of our bags and stuck to Igor like a tick at a campout for the next 4 days and 4 nights. I guess Igor felt sorry for us or took an immediate liking to us because he never made Dennis or me feel like we were an imposition. Somehow we got all four of us and a lot of luggage into Igor's Toyota SUV. If there were seat belts in that rig they must have slid under the seats. In the next few minutes, we began looking more intently for a seat belt. Igor, an energetic and intelligent businessman, jumped in the seat on the right, cranked up some awful music on the radio as loud as it would go, and we took off like a jackrabbit. For the next 20 minutes he drove with one hand as if we were being chased. He fielded about 5 lengthy cellular calls with the other hand, he gave hand signals to us since we didn't speak each other's language, and he was busy contemplating his next few moves in dealing with three crazy Americans. Then, when we got into the evening traffic of the city it got wild. In Vladivostok motorists arrive at extra large intersections where many streets come together and everyone gets out in the middle for a game of intersection chicken. There are no traffic lights or stop signs, no rules, masses of cars in the middle of the intersection jammed together like worms in a bucket, and everyone seems to know what they are doing. No one seemed to get upset; no one honked his or her horn, and Igor was working pretty hard going every which way to get through the intersection. He might be going south sometimes in the intersection to get north. It would take a few minutes to inch through each intersection—all the time he was working the cell phone. It was breathtaking if you have never experienced it.

Igor ran two businesses out of his downtown office, Kripto Tour and the importation of used Japanese cars. He always wore a nice suit but generally had no tie on. Businessmen and the women of downtown Vladi seemed to favor the pointed shoes. Igor always carried a brief case and he worked the cell phone like a pro. He was all business at—probably 30 years old.

We arrived at a "hotel" on the edge of town. The building obviously had plenty of age since it appeared to have a hundred coats of paint on the exterior. It was very colorful. Igor took us in and showed us three rooms for the three of us. Frederic was on a tight budget so price came up very quickly in the conversation. Igor said it would run us about $15 each per night for a room with a bed. As I recall, he had to write the number on paper, and it was a large number, but we figured that it was in rubles. The currency exchange at that time was 29 rubles to 1 dollar. Fortunately, the Russian numbering system looks like English.

Journaling at Igor's Hotel—Vladivostok

The shower was down the hall for Frederic and me but Dennis had one in his room. In fact, Dennis had a little frilly suite. For some odd reason we all wanted to know who owned the hotel and we later discovered, to our delight, that Igor owned it. We really felt like Igor was watching out for us.

The hotel was run by one female housekeeper for a 24-hour shift and then there would be a shift change. The housekeepers pretty much stayed in their small room about half way down the hall. There was also a stone-faced uniformed security guard that could not have been over 15 years old. I suppose his job was to look as mean as possible to scare anyone that tried to cause trouble. It was damp outside, if not down right muddy, and there was no pavement in sight. The three of us would track mud in the hallways quite often even though we tried to be very careful. The housekeeper would wipe down the entire 50-foot long and 8 foot wide hallway, on her hands and knees, about every two hours with a very strong solution of ammonia and water. I sure appreciate the scented candles of home after living under the heavy veil of ammonia for four days. Electricity is at a premium in Vladi so the hotel would use a 15-watt bulb where Americans would use three or four 100-watt bulbs. We didn't have hot water every night for the shower and there was at least a two-foot step up to the shower stall floor. You just climb in and fall out when you are done. The toilet was a real piece of art but at least it was indoors—carry your own paper though everywhere in Russia! I was always vigilant for varmints but I never saw one. So let's review, we had a housekeeper and a security guard that did not speak English and both had the facial expression of prisoners. There were no other residents but us three, there were dimly lit hallways and bathrooms, we had periodic hot water, there were no other amenities except a lonely pool table, and we enjoyed the constant aroma of ammonia. But I did not complain because I had a roof over my head, an indoor toilet, and hot water sometimes.

After we threw our bags in our rooms Igor loaded us up for a trip back into town. The road in and out of the hotel from the highway, probably five miles, was full of Olympic size potholes. To use an example, one particular pothole was on the east half of the road; if a Volkswagen fell in the hole there would be nothing showing above the surface—literally. The holes were everywhere. We knew that avoiding the potholes would be a real challenge for us once we gained control of our bikes again.

We were taken to a bank where I exchanged $700 for 20,300 rubles. That was almost enough to take me across Russia over the next 3 ½ weeks. This money was used for food, motorcycle insurance, customs charges, STS Logistics charges, a few hotels, and gasoline.

Still driving as though he was mad, or on an emergency run to the hospital, Igor took us to a book store so Frederic could get a map. There was never any talking when we rode with Igor. The three of us were speechless, breathless, and apprehensive about his driving and Igor was enjoying his favorite hits on the radio—at 120 decibels. Dennis and I are experienced travelers and proficient planners but we had no map and it never registered with us that maybe we could use a map also. We each had a GPS and we were relying totally on them—that thinking was flawed. Always, always, always take a map of the area.

Next, Igor took us to dinner and he had called ahead to ask an English speaking college professor to join us. Now I'm not a picky eater; the Marines taught me to not question my food, just scarf it down. We Americans all ordered something different and we all left most of our meals and it was not because we were not hungry. We split the bill three ways for the table of five at the upscale restaurant and the total was about 60 dollars, which was paid in rubles. On the way back to the hotel we stopped at a market so we could load up on snacks and drinks. Mostly we wanted bottled water and I added a Lite-Coke, and a sealed container of orange juice. That was the first of many bottled water purchases that contained carbonation—what we called gas. The unsuspecting first swig almost gagged me. It is really putrid tasting water but it will keep you alive in a pinch. It was a real challenge to figure out if you were buying the gassed water or the regular water. We made plenty of mistakes on that and we always paid a high price on the taste. I was looking for pork and beans in a can, peanut butter, smoked oysters in a can, canned tuna, or nuts. As far as we knew none of those items were ever available in Russia. Igor drove us back to the hotel, about a 15 minute ride, and told us a driver would pick us up in the morning about 8 AM. We were not sure what we would be doing but he seemed like he knew.

7

Red Tape in Russia

Dennis and I had a chance to talk toward the end of the day. I was getting very testy and irritated at everything. My GPS would not work, but of course I did not need it yet. Dennis wanted to help me and I was quick with him. The stress was building. We both agreed though, that the minute we landed in Russia, we knew we wanted out of the country and we only had 6,500 miles and 3 ½ weeks to go to make that happen.

After a cold shower I went outside and fired up the satellite phone in the rain, it was 9:30 PM in Vladi and 4:30 AM the same day in Goodland, Kansas. The first call to KLOE/AM radio went quite well and I had a lot to talk about. I could have easily talked on that tape for an hour. The tape was played on the Good Neighbor Hour two hours later. I was excited to think that I was talking with the folks back home, while I was a half a world away—even though it was a one-way conversation. My day concluded about 10:30 PM local time—I had crossed numerous time zones and lost a whole day over the last 25 hours. I left Denver on Saturday night; when I made the phone call it was Monday night in Vladi and only 25 hours had elapsed in real time. Our clocks work better than that in Kansas.

Tuesday May 18, 2004—*4:30 AM "I've been up an hour—probably eager to get started on the process of acquiring the bike from the Russians. Once we get the bikes we intend to get started toward Khaborovsk—833-kilometers north. I don't know how many days or hours it will take to get the bike; whatever it takes, that's what we'll give them!"*—From the Around the World journal

We spent the day on two issues. We finally met with a Senior Consultant with the Ministry of Foreign Affairs on registering our visas. There was some confusion on our parts on whether we needed to register and, if so, how often. The Senior Consultant's final recommendation was to register in Vladi and not worry about it again since we were going to be constantly moving across the country.

We thought we had the documents put together for customs so we could pick up the bikes the next day. The day went by really fast and there was very little spare time for the three of us—we were working on anything and everything that would help us get our bikes out of customs. John, the Kripto Tour driver assigned to us, was very patient with us. He was a very polite young college student that worked part-time for Igor. We wanted to talk to him but, once again, there was the language barrier. I had hot water that night and I got a good night's sleep!

There was generally a little time to go on an exploration walk in the mornings before our day of problem solving began. What was amazing about our rural neighborhood was all of the huge complexes on each side of our hotel. The buildings were abandoned and mammoth in size, maybe 100,000 square feet. It was not obvious what the buildings were used for in the past but it was obvious that they were designed for beauty and were quite flawed in their construction since they were in a dilapidated condition. Actually, there were just a few buildings in the area. The grass was grown up and very tall in the neighborhood; there was obviously no one taking care of anything. There was an unkempt statue of one of the former Russian leaders across the road and nothing around it but weeds. The backside of the hotel was adjacent to the bay of the Sea of Japan. The view of the bay was the only sight worth looking at in the neighborhood. I found the surroundings quite eerie in the daytime and spooky at night.

The next day of course, I was planning to pick up the bikes and start the ride. We spent ten hours working out the details of entry problems into Russia. We failed to declare at airport customs that we had an unaccompanied vehicle; we were told by the US Embassy fellow that it was unnecessary. Igor, through one of his many connections, managed to get us a notarized letter from the head of the customs department at Vladi accepting our apology and certifying the okay to let us have the bikes. John, our driver assigned by Igor, was hauling us all over Vladi to get these things rounded up. It was amazing how much time it took even with a knowledgeable driver. We bought our Russian liability insurance for the bikes and the cost was $32.58 for 30 days. Again, we worked on getting our visas registered and were unsuccessful since we were not staying in a "legitimate" hotel. We never did get our visas registered.

Five young people came over to the hotel from somewhere to shoot pool that night. They were drinking beer and generally having a good time and then they discovered me, the American. They had a lot of questions and only one of them could phrase a question in English. They really wanted me to try their beer, "The best in the world", they would say. They didn't understand the concept of being a non-drinker. Eventually, I reached for some gum in my pocket and they desperately wanted some. I had brought it from home and the brand was Trident. You would have thought I gave each of them a new computer instead of a piece of gum.

The next morning there was no hot water again, so this candy-ass took a sponge bath. Dennis and I were getting concerned about our GPS's not working since they couldn't locate the satellites. We eventually discovered that we had to manually input the new location in the GPS and they took right off; when you tuck them away in the dark and then fly them 8,000 miles they are confused when they see light again.

We spent nine hours working with customs to get the authorization to pick up our bikes. We will never know why it took so long but red tape is monstrous in Russia, do not get in a hurry. At 6PM STS Logistics of Vladivostok picked us up to take us to the bikes. We were getting excited until we got to the shipyard. There were sea containers in the yard everywhere the eye could see and they were stacked about 8 high—mountains of sea containers. I was sure they would not know which one was ours. I asked the driver how many containers were in the yard at that time—he said about 500,000, and my heart sank. Each container is roughly 8' wide, 40' long, and 7' high. The driver turned down one row, went about 50 yards and said, "Your bikes are in that one". Hot damn, I was about to get my Lucille back. I have no idea how they knew to have our container on the ground level, at that hour, with seven containers stacked above it. We watched with great anticipation, in the rain, as the gentleman cut the seals and opened the door. All three of us rushed the container to look at our bikes. "Mine's ok", yelled Dennis, "Lucille is ok", I yelled out, but Frederic was disappointed, he had a smashed windshield. He traced the damage back to some warehouse people in Tacoma, Washington and he eventually got compensated for the windshield. If someone were going to damage something on our bikes, the item we would choose would be the windshield. We all wear full-face helmets and a windshield is not really necessary.

It did not take us long to get our bikes unhooked and out of those containers and then we checked to see if all of our stowed gear was still on them—sure enough, it was all there. We put on our rain gear, fired up the bikes, and followed the STS man to the main customs gate so we could get out of the shipyard. We were as happy as kids at Christmas time. With the motorcycles in our possession, we felt free and liberated.

Goodbye! L to R Jim, Igor, Frederic, Dennis, John

The next hour was a challenge. The rain was heavy and the traffic through downtown was bumper to bumper-rush hour. John led us to a gas station so we could fill up. He pointed out a market so we could replenish our food and water rations for the ride the next day, then we followed him back to the hotel. Of course, I wanted to leave that night but it was impossible due to the risk of night driving in unfamiliar territory on top of the heavy rain and the poor road conditions.

We really had a fun evening. Everyone from Kripto Tour came out to the hotel and they fixed meat and dumplings—a favorite Russian dish—as a celebration of the Americans getting their bikes. They had more fun than we did because they were comfortable in the surroundings. Dennis and I were still on edge—it sure did not feel like home—but it was a celebration, just the same. I will forever be grateful for their intentions. We had been in and out of Kripto Tour ten times in the last four days and everyone was concerned about the welfare and the tribulations of the American bikers. All three of us tried to settle up with Igor. He had done so much for us by giving us a place to stay, furnishing us a car and driver for four days and making all the connections with government personnel to overcome our problems—he would take no money. That kindness and generosity will never be forgotten. Dennis and I believe the problems that we faced over the four days would have been too big for us to handle had it not been for Igor and his staff.

Frederic had planned to go around the world but at a much slower pace than Dennis and I so he was hanging back the next morning. He expressed no desire to ride with us due to our proposed mean pace. Dennis and I would leave the next morning. Igor and John were coming out to the hotel about 9AM to say goodbye—the bikes would be loaded and we would be ready to ride.

I was itching to get on the road and put Vladivostok in my rear view mirror and start racking up miles, or kilometers as they measure them in Russia. I do not want to give the wrong impression; there is nothing wrong with Vladivostok. In fact, it was one of my favorite cities in Russia. It is just that I am a motorcyclist at heart and that means I like my motor running and the wheels turning all day every day. I am obsessed with my passion of motorcycling. If I were not obsessed with the sport, I would not be spending thousands of hard earned dollars and taking two months out of my busy life for a semi-insane venture like going around the world on two wheels through waste lands—just to catch a dream. The people of Vladi worked very hard to make us comfortable for our short stay in their city. They went out of their way to help us overcome the obstacles of flying into a foreign country and obtaining possession of a motorcycle that came in by boat. The dream was out there on the road and it was waiting on us. I will be forever grateful to the people of Vladivostok. Thank you.

8

Robbery—First Day Out

The first day of riding in Russia was tough but that is part of the adventure. The day began with Igor and John coming out to the hotel from the city to say good bye. It was difficult leaving them since they were so kind and helpful to us. They were people that genuinely wanted to assist us in our adventure and they could see that we needed lots of help. Dennis and I developed a very special relationship with Igor and John even though our communication included no words. We had no idea how to deal with Vladivostok, customs, and the language barrier. After the customary pictures and handshakes Dennis and I were on our way north about 9:30 AM, riding around the outside edge of China. We understood that it is difficult to take one's motorcycle through China. It felt so good to be in the saddle again after being grounded for so long. I am totally at peace with the world, my God, and myself when I am on my bike. I give thanks generously to God as I ride. Some people would not fully understand those words. It is my belief that I am one of the fortunate few that have received the gift of a deep personal feeling for my God. I am not sure why God has blessed me so abundantly—I certainly do not deserve it.

One of the first things for us to encounter about 50 miles up the highway was a traffic control checkpoint. It was the first of many more checkpoints to follow. The checkpoints generally have a stout built cop hut beside the highway and a series of cones or barricades in the middle of the road for the drivers to negotiate. Naturally this slows the traffic down to a crawl. There would usually be numerous uniformed guards standing around. About one out of every two guards would be holding an automatic rifle at the ready position. One of the guards would be holding a black and white striped baton in his hand. The rule is, if he points the baton at you, the driver, you must pull over for questioning. Otherwise, you can continue right on through the checkpoint. They pull vehicles over at random and Dennis and I were random every time; most likely, because we stood out with our large bore motorcycles and our unusual attire. Rarely did any of the guards working the checkpoints know any English. That was an obstacle for them but it turned out to be a boon for us. Generally, they would ask some questions that were unintelligible to us and we would say, "English". They would ask some more questions and raise their voice a few decibels as if that would help us understand and we would say; "We speak English". By this time they were usually getting annoyed and would often just motion for us to carry on.

At the first checkpoint, I was through with the questioning and ready to move on in four or five minutes. Since no one there spoke English, Dennis and I were able to talk freely about what was happening to us. Dennis was beginning to unload some of his bags from the bike since he had misplaced his International Driving Permit that had a picture ID and a Russian interpretation of his Colorado license. I was beginning to get concerned since I had a GPS mounted on the handlebars and a satellite telephone in one of my bags. With extra time to kill I was afraid the guards would decide to have me start opening my bags. The guards were milling around my bike and really looking it over. Can we ever forget the potential of 10 years in a Russian prison for using a GPS in the wrong manner? We were beginning to laugh among ourselves at the stress of the situation and all the time silently wondering how sour this situation could potentially turn. As a distraction tactic, I did the only thing I could think of. I pulled out my digital camera and gestured that I would like to get a picture of all of them around the squad car. That was a hit. It took them a few minutes to get lined up, stow the automatic rifles, and recall their favorite pose. All across Russia, the guards would never let us take a picture of them with their rifles. I was really stalling with the camera by checking the sun, playing like I was focusing, and moving to different positions. All the time I was talking to Dennis, about 20 feet behind me, to see how he was coming on getting cleared. I had all of the other guards huddled up around one squad car and I didn't want to free them until Dennis was ready to ride. I was reminding Dennis periodically that I was cleared and ready to go. He was reminding me, as he was rather frantically looking for his document that he too would like to have clearance to leave before we departed since some of the rifles were trained on us. I finally said, "Try showing the guard your Colorado driver's license with the picture on it, he won't know the difference." It worked, and we were soon on our way and out of bullet range.

Traffic Control Checkpoint

The checkpoints were spaced about every 100 miles and it was not always easy to get through. Three times, I got ushered into the office for additional questioning. Once, the guard was fishing for a bribe but I stood my ground and he eventually released me. Another time, Dennis and I were both taken inside and after we were released I tried to take a picture inside the cop hut and that was a real no-no, as I quickly found out. A third time I was ushered into the cop hut with all my documents and handed them to the lady behind the desk. She looked them over, and then she looked at me and again at the documents, and said "ok"! I will never know for sure what really transpired at that cop hut.

We came upon a town and drifted toward an outdoor market. As we stopped, we immediately drew a crowd. This was common all across Siberia. Dennis nicknamed the swarms of people "locusts" since they would swarm on us very quickly. We used the term among ourselves until we got to Western Europe where we were unable to draw a crowd so easily. At the market we found vegetables and fruits, Coca-Cola, bottled water, yogurt, chocolate bars, small loaves of bread, and sticks of salami. We stocked up on these items and divvied them up to carry in our panniers in case we were hungry in isolated areas such as when we were camping at night. We checked out the smoking barbecue grill and found the old man cooking and marketing skewered meat. We each bought an order and it tasted pretty good with a couple of slices of bread but we had to eat fast. We didn't want to stay long since the crowd of people lurking around our bikes made us uncomfortable and we wanted to get out to the safety of the open road again and re-join the pothole Olympics.

It did not take me long to figure out that Lucille was my ticket out of the country. If Lucille would not carry me out, I was dead in the water without a paddle, thousands of miles from home, in a desolate country. There are many ways a bike can become disabled: theft, abuse, and normal wear and tear. Therefore, no one was going to mess with Lucille without an altercation with me.

Russia's road maintenance program is practically non-existent, especially in all of Siberia. Siberia takes up more than half of the largest country in the world. One has to be on guard at all times for threats to the safety of the rider and bike from obstacles, such as potholes that were imbedded in the surface of the road. There are no lines painted on the highways for safety like in America.

We had ridden about 500 miles, almost to Khabarovsk, when we started looking for a place to pitch our tents for the night. When camping we always wanted to be hidden and unseen so we could avoid the hassle of any drunks, thieves, and curiosity seekers bothering us through the night. We went to great lengths to find that isolation and sometimes failed to find a suitable tent site. There were very few roads leading off the main highway and it was mostly marsh ground beside us. Even with our dual-purpose bikes we could not negotiate the wet terrain for any distance, especially with our heavy loads. I finally spotted a muddy road going back into the woods so I started down it and Dennis followed me. Any kind of a side road was unusual so I thought I had found a real gem; it seemed too good to be true. The road got muddier and rougher each 100 feet and by the time we were a half mile back into the woods we were working very hard to keep the bikes upright and moving forward in the mud. Just about the time I was going to stop so Dennis could catch up, and we could talk, I glanced to my left and spotted what had to be a battalion of Russian Army soldiers with every eyeball on us. I had led us deep into the woods and to an army training ground. That situation made both of us very uncomfortable.

I kept right on moving to get away from the soldiers but I did throw them a Kansas wave hoping that would defuse the situation. I was hoping that Dennis would not have any trouble getting through that muddy area or we would both be in deep—. When I got a safe distance away from the soldiers I stopped so Dennis and I could discuss the rather tense situation. As I waited on him I noticed another company of soldiers up ahead and they were moving toward us out of curiosity. It was quick decision time; we had just a few seconds to make a big decision. Do we turn around and go back through all that mud again, and pass by the other group of soldiers to get out of there, hoping that both of us could make it through all the ruts? We were thinking and talking fast and the soldiers were moving in on us. The alternative was to keep on going, hoping that it wouldn't get any worse, and that the muddy trail would take us back to the highway. Within a minute or two the company of men was on us trying to ask us questions in Russian. The crowd was getting braver, closing in on us, and larger in size by the second. They were very curious having never seen large machines like ours before. I made a quick decision to keep going forward and hoping for the best. After some friendly gestures to the soldiers we took off; I began to pray that we were not getting in so deep that it would take the entire Russian army to pull us out. The traffic control checkpoints were enough to worry about in regard to the smuggled electronic equipment. At the time, the Russian army seemed like a larger concern to me.

We lucked out and made it back to the road in another mile. Sometimes when it gets a little tense I forget to breath. After a big sigh of relief, and short congratulatory remarks to each other for encountering the Russian Army and not causing international alarm, we were slinging mud off those knobby tires at 60 mph. We cheated death again!

We arrived at Khabarovsk about dusk, which was about 10 PM. Khabarovsk was the city where we would turn left, or west, cross the Amur River and engage in the ride of our lives. By then we were thinking about getting a hotel but how would one find a hotel? In Siberia, the hotels are not always on the highway. Hotels are not plentiful, the hotel sign would be in Russian, and they look like any other industrial building. So we just kept our eyes open and kept moving through the city of one million people.

Soon it was time for me to pull over and make the satellite phone call back to the states. We were still 17 hours ahead of the U.S. Mountain Time Zone at that point. The digital part of my watch was set permanently for the trip on mountain-time using the 24 hour military clock so I could tell if it was morning or night back home. The analog part of the watch was changed about every 2 or 3 days to fit the local time. Cold and wind had set in at Khabarovsk and as soon as I pulled into a parking lot we started drawing a crowd. We found out rather quickly, in Russia, that we had celebrity status with our large bikes and our unusual and somewhat expensive looking clothing. The people of Siberia had never seen anything quite like us.

As I was talking on the phone to KLOE radio I noticed I had a tiny red light on my chest like a laser beam and it stayed on my chest throughout the broadcast. I was getting concerned and many thoughts rushed through my guilty mind. Had the government somehow found out that Dennis and I had three pieces of unauthorized electronic equipment? Were they watching us with sophisticated equipment from an unknown location? We did find Russia to be quite paranoid about lots of things and I often felt an urge to run away from the situation, but to where, would I run? We felt like we were riding in a fish bowl with the whole country watching us. My concern at that point was understandable. Once again, the alarms were going off in my mind. I could visualize an armor piercing round coming through the air and being trained on my chest. After I finished the call to KLOE I zipped up my coat to prepare for the ride and I noticed that the light was coming from a small LED light that I had on my coat zipper. It must have been turned on earlier and I failed to turn it off. It had a white light or you could change it to a red light. The red light was on. A white light probably would not have alarmed me. Once again, the scare was over, this time a false alarm, and the pressure was off. I realized at that time that I was very untrusting of the Russian people and their government. As I look back, I don't believe they deserved quite that much distrust.

Drifting off course was a common occurrence in Russia since we didn't have any maps and we were too inexperienced with our GPS's to get the right assistance out of them. The first night was one of those times for losing our way. We couldn't find the bridge over the Amur River and we were wandering on our bikes through the large city. Finally, a young man who had been following us and watching us for some time realized what we were trying to find. He chased us down and motioned for us to follow him. We did and when he pointed to the bridge we gave him a big smile and another Kansas wave and he turned off. Then it was time to gas up. Without a hotel or a camping spot, we were forced to go out into the dark wilderness again, and who knew what lay ahead. At the gas station it was discovered that Dennis' left pannier was about to fall off. Upon investigation he noticed that some of the mounting hardware had come loose and fallen off. We spent about an hour trying different methods of repair and finally took it off. Dennis had to strap it on his seat with everything else. At that point we were both carrying four bags on the luggage rack and buddy seat and two new tires on top of all that. So the pannier was a real undesirable addition up on top, but he got by. Dennis had lots of weight on top and an imbalance of the panniers. That concerned me since his bike was really unbalanced and that is a definite no–no in motorcycle touring. We would just have to monitor the situation.

I learned quickly that it is very important to plan ahead when packing for a trip of this magnitude. A heavy-duty large luggage rack is a must if you are carrying lots of gear. In addition, forget the bungee cords. We were on a heavy-duty trip and that calls for heavy-duty tie downs. I used Helen-2-Wheels tie downs, 2 sets a piece in fact, and they work quite well to hold the gear in place—they are fool proof. The tie-downs, of heavy construction, will stay where you put them and if you weave the tie-downs through the gear it will not go anywhere. I also used Helen's soft bags, which are water proof, have loops built in for the tie-downs to go through, and they are made for motorcyclists. Even on really rugged roads the system worked very well; I highly recommend Helen-2-Wheels.

Fatigue had already set in; we were weary after everything that had happened throughout the day, and we already had 15 hours in the saddle. The stress load of the day was difficult to shake off because there was never a time when we could take a deep breath and just relax. Once again we were back out on the pot-holed road and we encountered rain to go with the darkness. The ride through those conditions, without highway paint striping, made it extremely difficult to navigate. A moon would have been welcomed that night. Then again, it may have been out and just obscured by overcast. It was Friday night and there was considerable traffic at 1 AM. One would assume that some of the vehicles had a drunk driver behind the wheel since vodka was quite plentiful in Russia. About 2:45 AM I could not stand it anymore; I had to pull over at a gas station to rest since I was falling asleep in the saddle. We got permission to park our bikes under the canopy of the station. Well, I "think" we got permission from the attendant—the glass at the pay window was deeply tinted and it was hard to see through. I believe there was a female on the other side of the glass but I'm not sure. We inflated my Thermarest mattress for insulation to sit on since it was about 35 degrees and we proceeded to fall asleep, in the dark, at the side of the building. A Thermarest brand, insulated and inflatable mattress, is the best-kept secret in camping. It provides adequate cushion, insulation from the cold ground, it packs easy, and it blows up in less than a minute by mouth.

It did not take long for a carload of intoxicated young men to spot our unusual bikes and come curiously to check us out. On second thought, it is possible that the station attendant called the drunks, after all, it was very late for them to be out "cruising" and there seemed to be no action anywhere. They wanted to converse with us but we just kept saying English, we speak English. I was still wearing my helmet; I tend to leave it on sometimes for warmth when I am resting temporarily. It was a chore to get rid of the curiosity seekers but we desperately needed some rest. Eventually they went away and we went back to sleep—a deep sleep. It was about an hour later when they woke us up again and, we later discovered, they had a plan the second time around. One person was to distract us with conversation and the other three would steal Dennis' helmet that was strapped to his bike. The talkative one was asking for my helmet, dollars, and rubles before he left. It seemed that the thing to do was to act stupid, which is easy for me to do, and to say "English" over and over. The others had what they wanted so they were honking for "Mr. Talkative" to come on so they could make their get-away.

After they left the second time Dennis and I started conversing at high speed to determine our next move and that is when we discovered the missing helmet. Losing Dennis' helmet was a bad deal for several reasons. It was a $450 helmet, the helmet allowed Dennis to see through the rain, it kept him warm, and his personal rights were violated. Dennis thought we should get on the road in case they came back a third time for everything else. I was concerned about going back out there on that nasty highway in the dark when we were so tired and it was full of potholes. Dennis said we could out run the drunks. I wasn't convinced of that since a drunk often has almost unlimited courage and we could only go so fast in the rain and the dark, with the potholes, before we were taking excessive risk. We did take off again at a fast pace and the drunks did not see us leave. We made it to the next town, Birobidzan, about dawn, 5 AM. What a way to begin a 10,500-kilometer trip across Russia—a 23-hour day jam-packed with physical, mental, and emotional stress. Maybe it would get easier. Dennis kept saying, "It can't get any worse, and it always did".

9

Amur—The XXX Road

Birobidzan is a pretty big city with plenty of commercial establishments. What we saw of the city was somewhat impressive, for Siberia. A drinking establishment that was just closing at 5 AM was in the middle of a staff meeting. I was immediately shocked since I could not imagine a staff meeting at 5 AM, at the end of a shift. I was immediately impressed though with the young tuxedo-clad crew. I was not seeing that well due to the fatigue but I approached them in full muddy motorcycle gear and asked if anyone spoke English. No one spoke up. Their bathroom, on another floor, was pointed out to me and I was about to leave when a young girl came up to me and said she spoke a little English. Those were the words I wanted to hear. It was good that she finally confessed her skill, even if it were limited in nature. What we wanted to know was where we could get coffee, some breakfast, and a hardware store for repairs to Dennis' pannier. She was eager to help us and took us next door where we could buy some weak coffee and a tasteless roll. We spent enough time warming up and drying off from the rain that the hardware store was just about to open. Once the pannier was repaired and we found a ski mask for Dennis to wear to keep warm, we took off again on about one hour total sleep over night.

Probably there are more people in Russia that know pretty good English than will admit to it. More than once, we found people who would finally admit to knowing some English if you could keep them around for a few minutes.

Birobidzan is the jumping off point for the Amur area if you are riding westbound across Siberia; that is where you leave the hard surface behind. The Amur is a very large swamp. The area is true Siberia with extreme poverty, very small towns, practically no commercial business, harsh winters and a high alcoholism rate. We estimated the ride across the Amur to be about 800 miles. It turned out to be 1,300 miles and there was less than 75 miles of pavement. Many motorcyclists over the years have tried to ride across it and, as far as we can tell, all have turned around rather quickly and put their bikes on the Trans Siberian Railway to get across the Amur. President Vladimir Putin announced in February of 2004 that the road across the Amur was *open* and Russia was now connected from Moscow to Vladivostok by road. What he was careful not to say was that it was *completed*. We grossly underestimated what we were about to undertake in the Amur. I nicknamed it the XXX road since I saw it as the pornography of all highways.

Heading north and west out of Birobidzan we began to encounter all kinds of very rough road conditions including: mud, ruts, washboard, sand, gravel, potholes, large jagged rock, hill climbs, dirt, shoe-flies around bridge construction and stream crossings. Often times the road was so poor and unmarked that we would just lose sight of it if we were going through town; the locals would point to another direction knowing that we were lost. They knew that there could only be one thing we were doing out there, trying to go cross-country.

The XXX road went through a few towns, mostly small in size, and they reeked of poverty. The houses were mostly black in color since they were neglected and, apparently, never painted. There were few cars in the towns we went through but many Ural Motorcycles with sidecars and some livestock wandering around unattended. The Ural Motorcycle is manufactured on the west edge of Siberia. Old, dilapidated Urals are everywhere in Russia. In town, residents put up makeshift fences around their properties to keep the livestock out of their yards. It is unusual to see a fence in the rural areas of Russia. The larger towns that we went through had railroad yards with an active high-decibel outdoor public address system to accommodate the Trans-Siberian Railroad. Each rail yard loud speaker system resembled what one might expect to hear in a Prisoner-of-war Camp. I often wondered what effect that public address system was having on the psyche of the public. It sure tried to drive me over the edge in listening to it for just a few minutes.

The dirt highway is where we started noticing the "Car Jockeys". These were people hired by used car import businesses to drive previously owned Japanese cars across Russia for re-sale to the unsuspecting public. The cars were taking the beating of their life getting across Siberia; it was like a lap-dance of demolition derbies. The elements of nature could rub and scrub on the cars but the cars could not touch each other. Many of the cars had cardboard taped on their front and lower parts for protection from flying rocks. We concluded that the tires, shock absorbers, front ends, and paint were pretty much destroyed on the trip across Russia. The car jockeys were very good drivers and they used the entire road, shoulder to shoulder, as we did, to avoid potholes, washboard, and deep mud. If one viewed the traffic from the air, not knowing what was going on, he would surely conclude that we were all drunk, mad, suicidal, or all of the above.

Ural Motorcycle with Sidecar

At first, the car jockeys were intimidating to us with their very aggressive driving habits. Later on we saw them as our friends, they became our cheerleaders, and we became just as aggressive with our driving. It was not unusual for them, or us, to be passing at high speed in mud or rock, and waving to each other during the pass. The traffic was virtually one way through the Amur. There was very little local traffic except for the car jockeys heading west and us two motorcyclists. Occasionally, we would encounter an Ural Motorcycle with a sidecar out on the highway. The car jockeys were driving mostly Honda and Toyota cars, SUVs and vans in groups of two to ten. In a day's time Dennis and I would pass the car jockeys numerous times and vice versa. They handled the loose rock better than us be we had a leg up on them in the mud and ruts. We were all stopping occasionally for food, gas, and coffee breaks. Of course, we could not speak to the car jockeys due to the language barrier, but we became friends through sign language and just seeing each other out there on the slow speed race track, day after day.

There is no question we were some of the very first motorcyclists to ride across Russia without using the Trans-Siberian railway—likely, the very first. There were two Australians ahead of us but they gave it up—more on that later. What we did not know was just how difficult it would be.

Cafes were spaced about every 30 miles along the XXX, and we stopped at many of them to get coffee, warm up, and generally take a break from the grueling ride. Reading the menu was impossible at the cafes and the waitress could never speak English. So, if there was no one else in there eating something that we could point to, we had to eat Borsht, a Russian beet soup, and drink coffee. The first bowl of Borsht is not too bad, but they serve it at every meal and the 20th bowl in 8 days is harder to get down. Often times though we could replenish our chocolate bars and Coca-Cola supplies at the cafes from the display counters.

Gasoline was also available but the quality was so bad that we would sometimes have to drain it out and fill up from a different pump. Dennis and I would intentionally fill up from different pumps hoping that one of us would find the "usable" gas. In all of Russia, you must pay for your gas in advance. Dennis and I had different methods of dealing with the gas station attendants. When I went to the window with pen in hand I would gesture that I needed paper to write on so the attendant would send out a piece of paper through the box in the wall. The box had a long rod on each end of it so you could pull the box to you or push it inside. I would write the number of liters of gas I wanted to buy and send the box inside. The attendant would write the number of rubles that she needed and send it back out. I would put the money in the box and send it in and she would send my change back out and turn on the pump for a certain number of liters. Once we got used to the way they do business we were able to comply rather easily … but it was rarely a cordial or friendly experience.

The locals were always a problem at the gas stations. We were always concerned that they might steal something off our bikes when we weren't looking. Once, when I turned to grab the gas nozzle off the pump to fill up the bike, I turned back around and a Russian soldier was on my bike and in the saddle. He just about got squirted with gasoline—intentionally. I came close to blowing up. You don't get on someone's bike in America without permission—you could start a small war by messing with someone's bike. The soldier must have seen the anger in my eyes as he leaped off Lucille. It is a good thing that neither of us made the wrong move—I would have surely lost that battle with the Russian government. The locals were often intoxicated when they came up to us regardless of the time of day or night. That made them more aggressive. Many of them offered us a drink of vodka and we always refused. They were usually taken back that we would not drink with them.

As we continued north and west along the only road available Dennis got a flat tire so we stopped and he plugged the hole. Dennis was getting the plugging routine down pretty good so we were soon on our way again.

May 22, 2004—We worked very hard that day and got a room about 5 PM since we only had about one hour of rest the night before. Finding the police station was the first order of business. As always, once the police department understood what we wanted to do with the bikes, they were quite accommodating. The plan was to get a room, unload our gear, and then take the bikes back to the police station for the night so they could lock them up for safety. Then we would walk back to the hotel. Often times, the police would give us a ride in the, always dilapidated, squad car. The room was okay and it cost us $10 each. Whenever we got a room we would unpack from the bikes and take our bags to the room one person at a time. We would never leave our bikes unattended. We got showers, had a dinner of lamb, I think, went for a short 10 minute walk, and turned in at 9 PM. We were literally in a deep sleep at 9:03 and the Russian Customs Officers knocked on our door five minutes later. They wanted to check our documents. They sure did not get a good impression of Americans since neither Dennis nor I could wake up to a full awareness. They must have looked at our passports and visas for 10 minutes; they made some notes and said goodbye. We could not have cared less what they said or did as long as they just left; we were exhausted. We got a good night's sleep that night.

Had All the Miles Been Like This We Would Have Never Complained

A Stop with the Car Jockeys Just Before the Road/Lake

A Road/Lake

Approaching at 60MPH—Don't Miss Your Line

Lucille at Rest

Our body and mind alarms went off simultaneously at 5:00 AM the next morning. The adrenalin was still flowing and both of us wanted to get back out on the road and keep eating that elephant one bite at a time to get across Russia. How else were we going to get out of those miserable riding conditions?

It was always a real hassle to get a room because we had to worry about the bikes. That morning we walked over to the police station just a couple of blocks away and talked the dispatcher into opening the 100-year-old padlock and the gate for us to ride out. Of course, it was all hand gestures again for communication.

The jail, directly adjacent to the front counter of the police station looked like something I used to see on the Cisco Kid movies back in the early 1950's and the movies were depicting something from back in the 1800's. The jail was tiny, dirty, dark, old, and smelly. A person standing at the counter might be grabbed by a drunk reaching out from the "slammer"; they were that close together. The mental depression that might set in for a "jailbird" in that jail would be punishment enough for the crime. The lock on the door of the cell looked like something from an antique store. In fact, what I have just described is the impression I got from the entire police station; it was very old, antiquated, inefficient, and it resembled America in the 1800s. I never really had a chance to internalize what I was experiencing and seeing, which was a good thing; I was always moving forward with my thoughts since I believed that was the safest way to approach the dilemma of being somewhere that seemed uncomfortable.

Back at the hotel, we started the process of hauling all the gear down from our second floor room, one person at a time, so the other guy could watch the bikes. Even though no one else was up at that hour, we just did not trust the bikes to be unattended. While one of us was going up after gear, the other one was strapping his last load on the bike. It would take at least 3 trips up and down the stairs for each of us since the four soft bags, the tank bag, and both new tires had to go up to the room the night before. That was the first morning to load the bikes after a night in a hotel. We are really efficient and skilled motorcyclists in my humble opinion. We wasted no time that morning, and it still took us 2 hours and 38 minutes from wake up to take off. In a camping situation, we were able to get that time down to no more than 30 minutes, and we saved just as much time by not getting a hotel in the first place.

Dennis "Runs the Rod" to Pay For Gas

Ah—Breakfast (Borscht & Coffee) Before Another Cold Ride

After a quick discussion about the direction of travel, I took the lead, as usual for this trip. Somehow we discovered, and not any too soon, that we were going the wrong direction. That mistake cost us one hour and 45 minutes. The wrong road that we took was of an asphalt nature but there were so many deep potholes that it was almost impossible to navigate. The potholes were very close together and, even at slow speed, one false move, and we were down. We constantly reminded each other, "Don't go down and don't get hurt".

On that day, we rode 323 miles. It was very difficult riding of treacherous mud, rock and plenty of potholes all day long. An evening dinner of 4 courses at a roadside cafe was a real treat; it included a beef patty, mashed potatoes, bread, borscht soup, pastry, and hot tea—all for $2.50.

Returning From the Police Impound Yard

10

Bike Won't Run

Arriving at the town of Shemanahuska about nighttime was all the encouragement we needed to look for a room again. By accident, we discovered the best way to find a hotel was to stop on the street, let the locals come up to us in a car or on foot, and motion that we wanted to sleep. They would quickly motion for us to follow and then they would lead us to the hotel, which is exactly what happened that night. We drew a large crowd, maybe 50 people, very quickly in the hotel parking lot. Fortunately, one of the members of the crowd spoke pretty good English. Dennis worked with him on negotiating a room with the owner of the hotel and I was to watch the bikes. It was difficult to keep an eye on both bikes and try to communicate with the crowd in some awkward manner. It was important that we parked the bikes side by side and pretty close together so I could protect them. I would position myself in the middle and to the back of the bikes and not move. Aware of the fact that the Russians in Siberia had never seen anything like us in their neighborhood, we tried to be polite and accommodating. The Russians that could speak English said we were the first motorcyclists to come through the Amur area. The Russians had only seen locals on the small, slow, dilapidated Ural motorcycles that were built in their country. The Urals never got very far from home and absolutely would not go cross-country.

Soon, Dennis and the English speaking person were back and I asked him how we could find the police station. He introduced me to the chief of police standing right beside me in street clothes. The chief had already called for a squad car to help us and we conveyed to him, through the interpreter, that we wanted them to lock up our bikes in their impound yard for the night and we would pick them up in the morning. They were very happy to accommodate us. So once again, we started hauling gear up to the second floor one person at a time while the other one was watching the bikes; we never had a hotel room on the first floor in Russia.

The officers in the squad car led us to the police station. The squad car looked like it was the winner of several demolition derbies. After getting the bikes secured for the night, the officers took us back to the hotel.

It was getting late in the evening, maybe around 9 PM, so we went next door to replenish our water, candy, soda, and yogurt supplies. We immediately attracted two soused ladies that were at the hotel bar for a party of sorts. The ladies followed us into the tiny market and showed us their prettiest liquored up smile they could muster. It was difficult to even move around in the tiny market with the ladies weaving and hovering over us. The market was obviously designed for one or two shoppers at a time. The ladies were trying to introduce themselves to us through the vodka and in the Russian language, to no avail. Fortunately, for us, their perturbed male friends rescued us from the inebriated damsels in heat. It would be difficult to adequately describe our mood at that time but it would certainly not have been one of "on the make". We were tired to the extreme, dirty, hungry for a decent meal, frustrated with the daily grind of the road, and not very sociable. We had two goals at that time, get out of the country and continue the mission of going around the world on a motorcycle. Shaking off discouragement was the task of the day—every day.

The next morning we retrieved the bikes, loaded up, had a nibble of nourishment from the panniers, and took off. We only went about a half mile and it was time to fill up with gas. After filling up, Dennis immediately discovered that his bike would hardly run. We started problem solving. We removed the gas tank, changed the fuel filter, and messed around for about an hour before a nice young gentleman came up and convinced us through gestures to push the bike over to the church courtyard so we could work on it in privacy. Once at the courtyard another gentleman showed up, obviously called by the first gentleman, and he proceeded to dive in to fix the bike. At first we were concerned about a stranger messing with Dennis' bike when we could not even communicate with him. I eventually convinced Dennis that I thought the guy might know what he was doing. The gentleman was a lumberjack, the pastor of the church, and a great mechanic named John.

It took John all day with plenty of trial an error fixes and contemplation but he eventually narrowed the problem down to diesel fuel in the tank rather than gas. The hoses at the fuel station were not marked well and Dennis had inadvertently picked the diesel hose to fill his tank. Once the problem was discovered we had the bike drained and re-filled with good gas in about an hour.

Courtyard in Front of Church—From L to R Caretaker, Deacon,
Lumberjack John the Mechanic

During the course of the day I ventured into a very small auto parts business out of curiosity more than anything else. I had five minutes to myself, and there was a new full-face motorcycle helmet sitting on the shelf. The attendant wrote down on paper that it was 486 rubles or about $18 U.S dollars. God had obviously planted one full-face helmet in all of Siberia since he knew Dennis would need to replace his that was stolen. Dennis bought the cheaply made helmet and it provided something to keep his head warm and the rain out of his eyes until he could get a better one somewhere in Europe. It was thousands of miles, in Munich, Germany, before Dennis would get a "real helmet" again.

The Russians were proud of their church facility. But, according to American standards, it was no better than one of our poor condition horse stables. All day long there were two church caretakers hanging around us. Their actions seemed weird, to me. One would walk with one leg and drag the other leg and he seemed a little spooky to me. The other fellow had more guts than sense. He was kind of quiet and always had a half smile on his face. One time, he had Lucille down on the ground before I could get my breath from gasping. I just wanted to sit on her, he gestured. Surprisingly, I kept my cool and I even helped him get her upright again so he could sit on her to have his picture taken. The two caretakers, I'm sure, were fine individuals but they were different. It was hard for me to feel comfortable with all of their goofy mannerisms, and that was my fault not theirs.

We took the two gentlemen to dinner that helped us, and we spent the night on the church floor in our sleeping bags but we kept one eye open for the caretakers.

The next morning it was time to ride once again. The diesel verses gas experiment had cost us one full day. The day began with 110 miles of large diameter loose jagged rock that consumed the first three hours. It got worse then, with the addition of potholes. There would be no peeling off heavy clothing that day since the temperature was right at 40 degrees all day and the sky was overcast.

Still, the riding was very tough on our bikes and on our bodies and quite dangerous due to the surface conditions. With all of the added weight on the bikes and the rough road conditions we were hitting bottom on our suspension quite often. I was real concerned that we might bend wheels or puncture tires. We worked very hard in the saddle that day, and we were up on the foot pegs for hours at a time, just to get 293 miles in 10 hours. It was discouraging to realize how hard we had worked in a long day to average 29.3 miles per hour. It was even more discouraging to think how much more of the tortuous road was ahead of us. With more personal fatigue setting in we called it a day at 4:30 PM. A room was found in the medium sized town of Skovorodino and the police kindly impounded our motorcycles for the night. As we were checking into the hotel, the clerk let us know that two other motorcyclists were there and had been there for three days. After getting settled we wandered down the hall to meet the other bikers. They were Australians and they were quick to tell us that the one stretched out on the bed had gone down in the jagged rock that we had all ridden through in the last 50 miles. The thick layer of sharp edged rocks the size of baseballs sliced him up pretty severely in the accident. His buddy got him to a nearby hospital with the aide of one of the car jockeys and the Russian doctors did a good job of stitching him up. What the Doctors could not do was repair his shattered courage. Down the road a thousand miles, we heard the Aussies put their bikes on the rail and headed home. They wound up as just two more casualties of the infamous Amur area of the Trans-Siberian Highway in Siberia.

The new day started out with 25 degrees on the thermometer and it sure did feel cold. The days were just cold enough to require thermal underwear and an electric vest all day long in addition to my windproof and rainproof Aerostich Darien jacket and pants. I rode with the Aerostich garments firmly in place everyday of the trip. They offered great comfort in inclement weather and protection in the event of a dreaded accident. The Aussie had just taken off some of his protective clothing before he went down in the rock. Afterwards, he admitted that was a big mistake.

The highway was not improving. It consisted of mud, potholes, detours through the creeks, some loose rock, but no pavement. Again, we did not make very good time—270 miles in 15 hours, or 18 mph, for an extra long day. The day was full of problems. Dennis had gone down in some mud along a tree-lined road. Fortunately for him, I realized pretty quickly that he was not behind me so I went back to investigate. He was not hurt but he needed a lot of help righting the bike before he could ride out of the mud. Just a mile up the road was where we thought would be a gas stop. We pulled into the congested station and discovered that there was only one pump. The electricity was off, and apparently, everyone needed gas. The curiosity seekers swarmed around us rather quickly and they were unusually aggressive. They were practically climbing on us, picking at the bikes, and asking lots of Russian questions, which we could not answer. It was about 3 PM and many of the curiosity seekers had been drinking for some time. We quickly decided to take a break, but away from all of the drunks. As we were leaving I cut a corner too short and Lucille threw me off as she went down. I caught some part of her with my leg as I was ejected and I clobbered my left chin pretty badly. It was a few weeks after the finish of the tour before that injury quit hurting.

Four Russian Boys Guard the Bikes While We "Dine" Inside

We went back down to the lake and had a snack out of our bags while we relaxed and discussed our options. The car-jockeys were taking a break there too so we just assumed a stop was in order. We were very low on gas and did not want to run out on the highway, in the middle of nowhere. The car jockeys assured us that there was another town about 30 miles away and it had gas. That would be a stretch for our low levels of gas supply but we had few options. After regaining some strength, we loaded up and went back to the one-pump gas station. Sure enough, the electricity was still off. We headed for the next town immediately.

We both made it to the next gas station with a huge sigh of relief and found a nearby cafe for some coffee and a meal. Four young boys took a liking to our bikes so we had them watch the bikes while we ate. After dinner we gave them a few rubles, a motorcycle card, and took their picture. They were real happy with meeting us Americans. The waitress in the cafe knew just enough English to tell us the next town was 40 miles and it should have a room. We were tired, as always in the Amur, but we headed that way. Arriving at the town, we just started looking for a hotel. I do not know why we thought we would recognize a hotel, but we were looking. It was getting late, about 9 PM, and pretty quick some youngsters on 100cc motorcycles started hovering around us. They led us to believe they would take us to a hotel. For the next 30 minutes they led us all over town like we were on a road race. It seems that Russia does not care how fast you drive. However, sometimes the police will pull you over and check your documents just for show.

We decided the kids were just playing with us and did not know where the hotel was located. At that point we wanted to rid ourselves of the kids; it was like flipping gum off your fingers. You can flip and flip and the gum is still there. After a series of quick turns at high speed we shook loose of the kids. I stopped in a neighborhood to converse with Dennis and a resident, speaking a little English, asked what we needed. "Hotel—sleep", I said. He said the town had no hotel. What a let down those words were to us weary travelers. You might as well have shot our tires off. We were very tired and our only alternative was to go back out to the highway and start looking for a place to pitch our tents. It was now 32 degrees, 10 PM, and the wind had kicked up to about 30 mph. After an hour of looking we settled on a site deep back in an active rock quarry. We pitched one tent for the two of us thinking that would provide a quicker get-away in case we were discovered by passers-by. That was wishful thinking. Lucille's clutch was now acting up and it would be a chore to ride out of the mud, ruts and hills of the quarry. We slept very soundly from 11:45 PM to 5 AM.

The 14 to 15 hour days of extreme riding were getting us down and really wearing on us. We were living on Borscht soup, coffee, chocolate bars, strawberry yogurt and Coca-Cola. The waitresses in the cafes could understand Borscht and coffee and we could see the chocolate, cokes, and yogurt sitting on the shelves at the tiny grocery stores. Of course we were carrying bottled water and trying to drink plenty. The long days did not leave much time for rest, maybe 5 to 6 hours. We were focused though. Each morning we would both pop out of a deep sleep right at 5 AM, without an alarm.

It became apparent as to why we were such celebrities with the locals in Siberia. Many others ahead of us had tried to ride across the Amur area, but they had all turned around to go back to the nearest town and put the bike and themselves on the train. The area is a big swamp and there was no official highway until 2004. Even then, it was simply "open", but far from finished. Therefore, the people had never seen anything like us. We were riding large overloaded motorcycles and we were dressed in $1,500 outfits from head to toe, for comfort and protection. We rode fast and aggressive—and we were foreigners to them. The locals wanted to know how old we were. Evidently, they thought we were too old to be taking a trip of that nature, 60 and 68. They also wanted to know how fast the bikes would go—the answer was, not very fast on the roads of Siberia but 200 kilometers per hour on the European Autobahns. The locals wanted to know where we were going. How do you tell someone you are riding around the world, starting and ending in Kansas, a state in the middle of the United States, when there is such a language barrier between you? We just started telling them Moscow. That sounded far enough away to impress anyone. What was interesting was the pronunciation of Moscow changing in the different regions as we went across the mammoth country. At first we could get the message across by saying musk-oh, and then we had to say musk-way, then musk-wa, etc. Once they realized we were going clear across the country, from Vladivostok to Moscow, they were really impressed.

I was disappointed in the lack of respect that the "locusts" showed for our personal possessions and our bikes. They would take things from our bikes if we were not looking. In all of my riding, that just has not happened to me in America.

11

Chita and Celebration

Chita, Russia is the west edge of the Amur area. We thought the highway would improve dramatically when we got to Chita.

We got in 149 miles one day and stopped 200 miles short of Chita to get some much-needed rest. There were just enough trees on a steep rise beside the road to offer us good cover from any passers-by. We set up our tents just off the road and began to endure the cold and the rain. While I was making my call back to the states for the radio broadcast Dennis was cooking up some noodles for our dining pleasure. Before I could get off the phone and take my first bite, a downpour filled my noodle cup with cold water. I dove into the tent; no dinner once again, just a chocolate bar. The cold was bitter that night but long-handles, socks, an insulated mattress, a sleeping bag, and a tent allowed me to sleep all night long. Actually, due to our fatigue, it was more like passing out than falling asleep.

May 28, 2005—My emotions are not the best tonight. I miss Molly, the comfort and the safety of Colby, Kansas, and the readily available water and clean air of home. I'm tired and cold, but I do not regret taking the trip—it truly is the trip of a lifetime.—From the Around the World journal

Expressing my feelings has never been one of my strengths and the world tour just drove that point home. In Siberia, I had huge diametrically opposed emotions going through me—I think. In one respect I was thanking God every hour for providing the trip of a lifetime to an avid motorcyclist. No question, this was the ultimate experience. On the other hand, there were plenty of feelings of guilt when I thought of the children and adults around the world that needed my financial and physical help. The money spent on the trip could have been used to help others. If I were accused of self-centeredness to the extreme, I would have no defense.

During that world experience I was at the point in life where I was questioning my purpose in life. "Why am I even here", I would ask myself. "What have I really accomplished"? Sure there was the achievement of 'honors' coming out of

Marine Corp boot camp which I shall always cherish. I will also take pleasure being elected to the City Council by a margin of one vote. There was the passing of the Series 7 securities exam and tens of other rugged securities, insurance, and designation tests. And then there was high achievement as a Caterpillar Heavy Equipment Salesman back in 1976. Working up to the top of the heap as a "Senior Financial Advisor" with a former broker dealer in 1995 was no small feat. But none of these items will mean anything after I am gone. So what is the real purpose of my life? I am searching and the answer is coming to me ever so slowly.

My mother went to the rest home with Alzheimer's disease shortly after my return from the world tour. Mom and I had never been real close, but we had mutual respect and love for each other. Mom was a real achiever. She was out there on the cutting edge of adventure as a young lady. Mom was working her way up the corporate ladder in the early nineteen fifties when it was not cool for a mom to be competing with men for income. The only thing that held mom back from great achievement was the juggling act of life. She had to balance her career, her family, and her personal desires. She sometimes dropped an object in the act but she would simply pick it back up and continue juggling. She was a very good competitor in the work world, and very successful, but she paid a great price on her relationship with her two children who craved her nurturing. I suppose every achievement has a price.

I can now see that mom had a big influence on me, and the way I approach life. I seem to be obsessed with getting all I can out of life. We only get one shot at living. God, I hope I still respect me when I get all done living.

Throughout the world tour I had these "zingers" go through my mind like racecars at the Indy 500. For two reasons the thoughts did not linger with me long: I had limited time to think outside of my focus on safe travel, and I did not have all the answers. Why not stay in denial?

We went down a lot in the Amur, that means we had accidents. Not only did that hurt our feelings, but also it was hard on our bones and muscles. Fortunately, we never went down at high speed or in the big jagged rock. As the fatigue set in, we had trouble picking up a downed bike—even with both of us lifting. I weighed Lucille at the local Coop just before the trip started, as she was loaded for the trip with me in the saddle. She weighed 1,000 lbs.

Dennis shared with me one night that he would have turned the trip down had he known what he was really getting into, but he never complained during the trip. I did not know either, what we would encounter. I just figured it would be difficult. If a motorcyclist tells another motorcyclist the road is real tough to get through—what does that mean? The answer is it depends on the experience, skill, and expectations of each rider. Siberia is real tough to get through.

About 60 miles from Chita we came upon pavement. Thank you Lord for hard surfaces! I was never so glad to see a hard surface in all of my life. A second exciting encounter at that point were the tens of car jockeys that had pulled over and stopped along side of the road to wave us across the finish line of the XXX road. They knew we were right behind them that day and they wanted one more friendly wave with us. What a marvelous momentary celebration they provided. We had one of those ear-to-ear grins and we waved vigorously to them like brothers completing a tour of duty at war. The Russian Car Jockeys, with their mysterious Russian tongues, are the only people in the world that know what Dennis and I really endured during those eight days in May of 2004. They seemed to be proud of us Americans. Actually, the car jockeys have to work quite hard also in their "caged vehicles" to get across the Amur. Thanks men for your support, we will always remember our unspoken camaraderie!

We were at a roadside cafe and a drunken trucker really startled us for some reason. Dennis and I were taken aback when we noticed the drunken semi truck driver climbing into his rig to take off again. He wanted us to join him for some "wadka". Of course, we just tried to ignore him.

I suppose the drunken driver made us recall the accidents that we had observed across Russia. When we saw an accident in Russia, and we saw several, they were always fatal. Head-on impacts, no seat belts, and vodka prevented the occupants from surviving. The Russians are very good drivers when they are sober but not so good when they are drunk—and that is not unique to Russia. A couple of days before, we had gone through an accident scene early in the morning. Two truckers had hit head-on in the night. Their covered bodies lay beside the trucks as we passed by. The road was bad, and one could not take it very fast, but the accident victims still died in the accident.

Hello Chita! What a beautiful sight that large city was to us. We had some errands to run since we were back in civilization. We needed nuts and bolts for Dennis' panniers again and we needed to replenish our food and water supplies. Finding those businesses was no easy task due to the size of the city and the language barrier. At an outdoor market we left our bikes unattended for about 10 minutes. That was too long. Someone reached into my tank bag and pulled out my GPS, even with a crowd around him. That theft cost me my $250 GPS for the rest of the trip and the only piece of navigation that I had with me. We really missed the information provided by the GPS and the thief would not even know what to do with the gizmo.

Dennis resting on "Lucille"—Camping at Chita, Russia—The Singing
Power Line was Overhead.

We wanted a shower and a bed but we opted to go out into the woods again due to the hassle of securing the bikes. As we were leaving town I noticed the cutest cafe along side of the road and they had the grill going outside. That meant there would be meat that we could point to for dinner. We dined on Shish-ka-bob, 2 cups of coffee, salad, desert, and bread for $4 each. The entire staff at the cafe was in awe that two Americans had stopped at their cafe. As we ate our first good meal in eight days, at least 10 staff members hovered around us bombarding us with the best English questions they could muster. Actually, one young waitress knew most of the English and she did most of the interpreting for the others. She gave me a 49-cent lighter before we left. Dennis said I was to give her something so I gave her one of my $1.50 business pens. I could tell she wanted more. As I was leaving she had spotted my $9.00 LED light. I had never used it yet on the trip and she will cherish it forever so I made her the proud owner.

We continued west out of town and soon found a good spot to camp in the woods under a major power line. We had more time to ourselves that night than usual. There was about an hour available before bedtime, which gave us some time to repair our bikes and gear, before a three-hour rain developed. About 1:30 AM I heard some loud music and I was sure we had been spotted by some drunken youth. I was getting alarmed. Being spotted, at that time of night, would be our worst nightmare. It was crazy music, almost a monotone. Then again, it seemed like all Russian music was crazy to me. I peeked out of the tent and did not see anything but the music went on and on for about 20 minutes. I finally concluded that the power line was singing to us. It was eerie, and I never want to hear that song again. May 30, 2004—We were heading west out of Chita and on pavement—whoopee! It was Sunday and the ride was fairly uneventful that day. We arrived at Ulan Ude, a large Siberian city, and we needed a room. A guy in a car stuck to us like glue in town and finally started honking his horn and motioned for us to follow him. Somehow he knew what we needed and he led us to a nice hotel. Dennis went inside to negotiate a room while I stood guard over the bikes. There was considerable commotion outside from people coming and going and one of the bystanders was an English speaking Russian gentleman of Japanese heritage that struck up a short conversation with me. It was sure comforting to speak my language with someone besides Dennis. The young handsome gentleman, whose name was Batar, was an attorney from Moscow, over 4,000 miles to the west. He was in Ulan Ude managing some details with local governmental officials for his family's construction business. He was obviously polished and quite wealthy. We paid a lot for the room that night, $33 each. We still had the problem of securing our bikes. Batar came out of the hotel again and asked if we needed some help. I explained our dilemma with the bikes and he suggested that we follow him across town and he would lock up the bikes in their construction yard and have one of the hired hands guard them all night. We wondered about getting the bikes the next morning. He said he would be at the hotel at 7:30 AM to take us to the bikes. He also scolded us for trusting a Russian. He said "you can trust me but do not trust other Russians". We promised to be more careful. Batar became our friend in a short period of time and we are very grateful for him going out of his way to help us—the strangers from America.

We really needed to do our laundry. We had been out about nine days from Vladivostok, had ridden through some of the toughest wilderness riding that Asia has to offer, had mud and oil all over us, and we had washed nothing but ourselves, and that was done very crudely. A couple of ladies with the hotel crew came to our room and looked at our laundry piles before quoting us a price of $21 each. Dennis tried to negotiate down the price but the ladies stuck to their bid—I was proud of them. The gals did our laundry through the night, had everything back to us at 6 AM, and it all looked like brand new. We feel like we got a real bargain and the gals had never made so much money in one night. That morning we looked like civil people once again.

The hotel in Ulan Ude provided us with many memories. While I was in the parking lot waiting on Dennis to get our rooms, a lady came up to me and said, "where are you from"? I was startled because she was speaking my language. I said, "America". She said, "I know but what part of America"? I said, "Well, I'm from Kansas"! She said, "We are from Iowa"! Now here I am about a half a world from home and I run into someone that is practically a neighbor. The lady and her husband were in Ulan Ude for the third time to adopt a baby girl and, this time, they were taking her home. They were so excited and Dennis and I were excited for them. We saw their bubbly faces several times during our 14-hour stay at the hotel but we only saw pictures of their darling Russian soon-to-be daughter.

With a westerly heading again the next morning, we quickly ran into another traffic control checkpoint. This one was larger in scope, with several lanes, and the cop office was two stories tall. The traffic was really backed up at the checkpoint. We never did discover why. When Dennis and I worked our way to the front of the line we had to park our bikes and go into the office with all of our documents. The harsh appearing lady combed through our documents very slowly, looked us over thoroughly, and finally turned us loose. We never knew what that was all about but we were the only ones that got "called to the office"; some things in life are just never answered.

It was a sunny, brisk, and beautiful day to ride—even in Siberia. We went around the south end of Lake Baykal at 70 miles per hour. If one were on vacation, a stop-over at Lake Baykal would be a must. The lake is the deepest fresh water lake in the world at one mile in depth. The lake was quite beautiful, peaceful looking, and inviting. We went by at high speed but we observed no activity on the parts of the lake that we saw.

Turning back to the northwest at the south edge of Lake Baykal, we were heading toward Irkutsk, still on pavement but not such good pavement. In one particularly rough stretch, filled with potholes, Dennis and I both lost our rear brakes within a mile of each other. The same banjo bolt had loosened on both bikes; a stranger thing will never happen. We were carrying some brake fluid so we topped off both master cylinders and proceeded to bleed the brakes. Lucille cooperated and I had my rear brake back in no time. Dennis, on the other hand, had a broken part in his brake system. He was forced to ride without a rear brake for the next 4,000 miles until we could get to a repair shop.

That afternoon, I received some bad gas at a filling station. Lucille did not like that gas and she coughed and choked and sputtered. No question, I would have to drain out all of the gas and refill her from the pump that Dennis used. After an hour of messing with that gas and getting it all over us, we were on our way again. I tried to get my money back for the tank of gas that I drained out on the ground but the cashier put on a good show of acting like she did not understand so she could avoid paying me. I called her a few choice names under my breath and left.

Monday May 31, 2004—*We had difficulty finding the highway through towns since it is not marked at all. I was so tired after only 4 ½ hours of sleep that we had to stop for a 15-minute power nap.*—From the Around the World Journal

We discovered that we could get by a lot better in the afternoons if we took a power nap as soon as one of us got really tired. We would find a decent place to pull off the side of the road where people would leave us alone, we would put the bikes up on the center stands, jump on the saddle, lay our head on the tank bag and go into a deep sleep. We would wake up simultaneously 15-minutes later and be on our way again. I would usually just leave my helmet and gloves on since it offered a quite comfortable environment to sleep in. Most afternoons for us in Russia included a power nap.

Tuesday June 1, 2004—*Lucille is running very strong—very fast—and all systems are working. She has taken a terrible beating and just asks for more. Dennis still has no rear brake on his bike and all of the oil in his telescopic front end has leaked out. We have both seen enough of Russia and we are only half way across. Russia, Siberia, just does not offer enough for tourists; it is very remote and 80 years behind America.*—From the Around the World Journal

We started looking for a secure tent site around 5:30, and it was 7:30 before we found a suitable location. It was raining most of the afternoon. In the rain, Dennis fixed us some tuna and noodles for dinner. It wasn't first class food, but it was warm and chewy.

As usual, we rode for awhile after we broke camp before stopping for some breakfast the next morning. We came across a really nice roadside cafe and it looked as though everyone else had discovered it also. There were many car jockeys in the cafe, so we were able to point to some food that we wanted to order for ourselves. The meal was very pleasant even though we spoke no one's language in the cafe.

When we came out of the cafe we discovered that Dennis had a flat tire. He probably picked up a nail but we did not even check to see. I said, "Dennis, this must be the day that we change out our tires". He agreed, and we got started. We pulled our bikes off to the side and began the task of changing our four motorcycle tires. Our "knobbies" were mostly worn out. I had hauled a bead breaker, two tire irons, and a battery operated air compressor, half way around the world, just for this task. We had carried two new tires all the way across the Amur area since we were sure the roads would eat up our tread in no time. We got 3,690 miles out of the new Metzler Karoo knobby tires that we had installed in Tacoma, Washington. We were thankful for that performance considering the abuse they took. We had ridden in so much jagged rock that I was amazed we did not have more problems with the tires. We were putting on Metzler Tourance tires, which had a universal type of tread. The Tourance tires carried us on home and then some. I got over 10,000 miles out of the Tourance tires, partly because the roads had improved dramatically, and partly because we kept our speed down to a respectable 70 mph except for the few miles that we were running fast on the Autobahns of Europe.

Dennis was concerned about us being able to change out the tires ourselves since he had some trouble one day getting a bead over a rim. We really did not have any trouble but it took us 5 ½ hours to change the four tires. That cafe got two meals out of us. For awhile, I thought they might get a night's stay from us also.

Lucille Getting New Shoes

When we finished the tire changing, got cleaned up and fully loaded again, we took off. It was like we had new bikes. First, we were not carrying two tires on top of everything else any longer. Secondly, we had universal tread rather than knobby tread, and third we were running on a hard surface. The universal tread corners better and gives a much smoother ride on hard surfaces. I was so happy; I could hardly contain myself. The trip was getting much easier by the day, and I was smiling more. I was living the dream!

12

Fatigue, Vodka & a Gift

It was still very cold every day, especially in the mornings. On June 2 we went through Krasnoyarsk but not without asking directions a couple of times. Again, the highway was unmarked and we kept losing it among the city streets due to poor signage, or no signage. After leaving the cafe that morning, I went the wrong way. That cost us 85 miles, round trip. My compass and GPS had been stolen and I was dependent on both of them. We did have a map, but it was in English and all of the signs were in Russian. I could not even guess what the Russian signs meant.

We spent that night in a hotel at Maureensk, RU. Even the police did not want our bikes out of our immediate possession unless they were locked up and out of sight. "There would not be anything left of them—in no time", they said. The hotel owner took a liking to us and so did his brother. The brother allowed us to lock up the bikes at his home just across town. He wanted to ride Lucille over to his home. He had never ridden a motorcycle, but he was trying to convince me that he could. There was not one chance in 100 that he could have ridden Lucille beyond our sight distance without an accident—and likely a bad accident. Lucille would have thrown him off within 25 feet, so I said no as gently as I could.

We had a nice big room with three beds; we were enjoying the thought of all the extra space. A little later, we finally understood the owner to say he would be in the third bed. That appears to be a common practice in Russia. One rents a bed—not a room.

The next day we went through Tomsk and Novosibirsk. It took us an hour to get through Novosibirsk due to heavy traffic; it was not fun. Lucille was running strong and doing her best to give me a comfortable and dependable ride. On the highway, Dennis had a pannier come off and he lost a lot of gear out of it. He decided to just throw the Jesse Bag away. Dennis' bike, which had 30,000 more miles than Lucille, had given him more trouble on the trip than my motorcycle.

The rear brake was now out, the oil in the front forks had all leaked out, his ABS braking was out, both right turn signals were gone, he just lost the right pannier, and the left one was cobbled on with makeshift bolts. At this point I was encouraging Dennis to put his bike on the Trans-Siberian Railway and get it, and himself, to Germany to get the bike fixed. I felt like I could make it solo okay and I could catch up with him again in Germany, but Dennis wanted to ride the rest of the tour.

Thursday June 3, 2004—*We are camped out beside the highway—the mosquitoes are thick and the flies are as big as 1ˢᵗ year quail.*—From the Around the World journal.

Friday June 4, 2004—*We broke camp at 5:35 AM. We immediately got gas and went to the cafe that was close for coffee and borscht. We rode 500 miles today and it was 97 degrees as we rode the stop and go traffic of Omsk; it was very hot. Lucille acted up at the last gas stop. I filled her to the brim and she was leaking out of the vapor recycle canister. We pulled the hoses and drained the canister and she ran much better. Now her tachometer wanted to act up. We camped out about 150 miles east of Tjumen and it started raining as soon as we had the tents set up. We are both really ready to get out of Russia. There is nothing here to come back to see. We both agree that it is very dangerous to ride a motorcycle across this country, especially if you are going to ride the Amur.*—From the Around the World journal.

Saturday June 5, 2004—*We were on the road again at 6:20 AM. The mosquitoes were plentiful last night, but we did not have any in the tents after we strangled the two or three that rushed in when our doors were open for just seconds. Today, it was very cold, dark, overcast, drizzly, foggy, and 50 degrees; I loved it.*

The towns are using lots of roundabouts for traffic control at intersections. They seem to be a very efficient way of getting vehicles through the intersections without the wait times of traffic signals.

Most buildings for the last 5,000 miles have had no indoor plumbing. At cafes we wash up from a basin in the dining area that has a plunger spigot providing a couple of drops of water from the tank above when you palm the spigot; the staff keeps the supply tank full. If I write a book I need to discuss: **Safety**—*have good tires; consider ice, rain, and snow; tie extra gear on very well; wear a full-face helmet; wear protective clothing; wear water proof everything (which helps with the wind also); have a good battery; carry a heated vest; know how to handle panic stops; know how to abruptly negotiate around obstacles; have reflection on the bike, the helmet, and the clothing. As far as* **Comfort**—*have a good seat and proper seat height relative to your skill level; make sure the tires have good tread and are in good condition (for comfort & safety); make sure the windshield, if an add on, works well for the bike; have plenty* *of engine power for tight situations; suspension should be adequate for the load and riding conditions; good—no great—brakes are a must; know the risk that one is taking; ask plenty of questions about weather and road conditions. Finally, for* **Fun**—*look for tree lined highways with curves and hills; use the crisp mornings for great feelings; catch the aromas off the fields; make speed your friend but stay within your skill level; watch speed as your enemy in tight situations; acceleration in the right situation is fun; enjoy the togetherness with your significant other.*

It was very cold today, even with the electric vest on. In late afternoon the temperature was 34 degrees, we rode in hail, snow, and rain; it was generally miserable riding. We are about 1,200 miles east of Moscow. We could not find a suitable hotel with good security for the bikes so we found a place out in the cold wet timber to pitch our tents. This would be the third night in a row for camping. Yekaterinburg, former President Boris Yeltsin's hometown, is about 50 miles behind us and it did have a better first impression than the other Russian cities that we had seen.

It is very cold in my tent but I think I will be ok in my sleeping bag; I may have to leave my socks on for warmth though.

We are pushing very hard to get out of this country it just doesn't feel that good to us. We stopped at a small cafe for a late lunch today and they were grilling shish-ka-bob out front so we were looking forward to the treat of a leisure hot meal. We could not even enjoy lunch because a motorcyclist convinced us that the locals were watching us. He said they would steal from us in a heartbeat and run with the goods. We ate in shifts and left quickly.—From the Around the World Journal

Sunday, June 6, 2004 *Again, we rode in 34-degree weather this morning, it was very cold, and we could only get 150 miles behind us in the morning due to the cold. We did have a great Mexican lunch in Perm—believe it or not! It was as if God just planted a Mexican restaurant in Siberia for us as a treat. The restaurant was in the lower level of the building and it was decorated just like you might see in the states. The food was as good as something you would find in Denver and I was able to get my diet Pepsi, chips and salsa, and a burrito. We had not eaten like that since leaving home three weeks ago. The meal cost $25 dollars for the two of us (very expensive in Russian terms) and I would have paid twice that much.*

The countryside is quite beautiful now but you would not dare stare too long at the landscape while moving for fear of ending up in a pothole. Every moment of riding across 7,000 miles of Russia is fixated on the road surface directly in front of you whether in a town or in the country. There is, apparently, no road maintenance program in most of Russia—at least we didn't see any equipment in the last week of May and the first two weeks of June. One could get in big trouble real quick by tangling with one of those potholes.

The Villages are Looking Better Now

So far we have been stopped, other than for traffic control points, four times by the authorities. Each time we were speeding excessively and all they would do is look at our documents and turn us loose. It was rather frightening at first since we could imagine all kinds of bad things happening to us if stopped, but later we got used to the stops—actually, we got a little cocky.

We are getting the traffic control point stops down to a science. I am usually leading; I tell them I am American, and I only speak English. They rattle off a few comments or questions in Russian and I say, "I only speak English". Frustrated, they usually pass us through. One time I was taken into the office for no motorcycle endorsement on my International Driving Permit. I tried to show the officer that it was an oversight by AAA, the issuer, since my Kansas driver's license showed an endorsement. What he really wanted was a bribe since he mentioned, "you businessman—I businessman". I did not bite on that BS, so he eventually let me go.

We could not find a suitable place to camp since the fields had water standing from recent rains. I took us through a small village and headed for the tallest building, a beautiful church with a gold colored dome. We stopped in the middle of the intersection with our engines off to problem solve our sleeping quarter dilemma. We sat there for the longest time and two ladies eventually had the courage to come investigate the two motorcyclists visiting their village. The language barrier was at its greatest level with these two ladies; we could not even gesture what we needed—a place to stay or a place to pitch our tents. It took about 45 minutes, but we finally communicated that we would like to pitch our tents in the church parking lot for one night and we needed nothing else. They got permission from the priest who was out of town for the moment, and we began setting up camp. We had an outhouse just about 50 feet away so we had everything we needed for camping in a village.

Pretty quick one of the ladies showed up with lemonade and bierocks for a snack; she will never know how much I appreciated the food. Soon six middle school age girls found us and became infatuated with the "Westerners". They wanted our pictures and autographs, which we were delighted to provide. About 10 PM, it was time for us to get some rest, but it was very light and the girls were still milling around staring at us. Reluctantly, we ran them off and they came back about 10 minutes later with a nice picture of all of them posing in someone's nice home. I will not forget the young impressionable girls; they were real cute and like a breath of fresh air.—From the Around the World journal.

We slept well on that piece of slab that night. When I was planning the trip I was concerned about all of the animals I might encounter in Russia. Of course, I had heard about Siberian Tigers. A little research suggested that there aren't very many Siberian Tigers in existence. Beyond the tigers, I did not know what to expect in the way of animals—maybe some wolves, snakes, spiders, muskrats, etc. The really interesting thing to me was that we did not see one wild animal of any kind in all of Russia except birds. Dennis said, "They ate them"! That would be a lot of eating; it's a big country—but I think he may be right.

The difficulty in locating a tent site each night was the marshland and the lack of roads off the main road. We would often look for hours as we traveled trying to spot a secure site. Once we located a suitable site we would have our tents up in seven minutes and we could literally be asleep in a total of 10 minutes if we were that exhausted—which we normally were. We had good camping gear including tents that would stand fairly high winds, heavy rain, and the threat of invading mosquitoes. Our sleeping bags were pretty comfortable down to 20 degrees. The thermal air mattresses though are the key to comfortable camping. They kept us insulated from the cold ground and provided adequate cushion to allow a deep sleep. Each of us carried a headlamp like miners wear for navigating in the tent, around the campsite, and writing in our journals. We never left our tent doors unzipped and once inside there were only one or two mosquitoes to execute. After "camping" in the Marine Corp, I told myself I never wanted to see the hard ground again. But camping gear improvements have come along way in the last couple of decades and camping now can be a pleasant event with proper planning.

The poverty in Russia/Siberia is extreme but the people seem to be okay with it—but then again, they have vodka to soothe their pain. If I had to live there very long, I would need a lot of depression medicine too.

I need to clarify something. I am writing just as I saw it and just as I felt it—that was the trip. Never once did I regret taking the trip, so I am not complaining about the circumstances that we found ourselves in at times. I knew going into the Around the World trip by motorcycle that it would consist of the good, the bad, and the ugly. That was all part of the dream.

Monday, June 7, 2004—*It just seems like it is taking forever to get to Moscow! The towns and villages are getting closer together, they are bigger, and there is less poverty showing. For lunch, we stopped at a large roadside market where most of the venders were selling barbecued fish, the whole fish. We now are encountering tour busses, and they are stopped at this market to let everyone stretch. Tour busses out of Moscow and St Petersburg must go out east a way but certainly would not go into eastern Siberia; it is too primitive and too desolate. Dennis and I were the big hit at this outdoor market today. Dennis has a video segment of me trying to give an impromptu seminar on Around the World motorcycle travel to a large group of people that had no idea what I was saying. Everyone was laughing and having a good time. It feels good to be a celebrity, even if it is brief.*

The Ladies Brought us Lemonade & Bierocks

We opted for a hotel room—what a hassle to get a room and secure the bikes at the police station. The police offered to haul us back to the hotel in the "squad car". What a joke! The passenger side patrolman had to hold his door shut or it would fly open, it needed a muffler, and the interior was shot. The driver patrolman was hopped up on something and wanted more vodka. He turned to go toward the liquor store and we convinced him that we did not need any and we were not buying him any either. So he did the next logical thing and stopped to visit with one of the local prostitutes along the side of the street; he wanted to offer her services to us. I do not know if Dennis and I just looked like unscrupulous bastards or if he treats all newcomers to town with the same respect. The chief at the headquarters seemed like a nice guy with some scruples. But he obviously had one loose canon in the department.—From the Around the World journal*

Back at the hotel we discovered that we had to haul hot water for our shower. We would pick up a couple of gallons of very hot water at the office and take it to the room. We then simply had to stand on a chair and pour it into the supply tank up above the showerhead, pull the chain, and enjoy.

The next order of business for the night was to eat dinner at the hotel restaurant. I was looking forward to a relaxing dinner in a commercial atmosphere. I envisioned a great warm meal and something cold to drink. The restaurant looked clean, fairly modern, and fairly quiet since there was hardly anyone in there. I thought we were really getting into a good experience—no such luck. We had trouble ordering from the menu, so we ended up with marginal food at the best. For our dining entertainment, a mother daughter team of diners danced for "their" enjoyment. The mother was very drunk and the daughter had her hands full trying to contain her. After dinner the police chief came by the hotel with a friend that knew English. He was so excited to practice some of his English on us, and we were delighted to speak our tongue to someone besides each other. He asked us if we needed anything. I said, "We could use a map since ours is in English and the signs are in Russian". He looked perplexed like he was going to have trouble locating a map.

The next morning, bright and early at 6 AM, the chief and his friend came by the hotel to take us to our bikes. The friend had no less than a Russian Atlas with him that he had signed and presented to us. We thanked him very kindly for his efforts and his thoughtfulness. At the police station one of the caretakers sheepishly asked 13 Rubles each from us for watching the bikes all night. We agreed to pay him the 40 cents he was asking. After picture taking with the chief, his friend, and two other officers, we were on our way again.

L to R Dennis, Friend of the Chief, Police Chief, Jim

Tuesday, June 8, 2004—*We rode very fast most of the day, but at 2 PM we went through 10 miles of road construction—and I mean right through the middle of it, with heavy traffic. It is now 3:45 PM and we are just 150 miles from Moscow.*

We went into Moscow and promptly had a well-deserved McDonald's cheeseburger, French-fries, and coke—they tasted the same in Moscow as they do in Colby, Kansas. For bike security we ate the meals on our bikes at the curb. The pedestrian traffic was heavy as well as the vehicle traffic—it was about 8 PM. While eating, we were amazed to see an elderly couple approach their car so drunk they could hardly stand up. No one seemed to care that they were going to drive drunk.

It was difficult to get someone to admit they knew a little English so we could ask them where Red Square was located. We were asking everyone that walked by if they spoke English. A young girl was finally encouraged by her friends to help us. She did a good job of directing us in her second language, English, and we were there in minutes. After the ritual pictures of each of us in front of Red Square, we were off again—about 8:30 PM.

We rode west and waited too long to find a campsite. It was dark, raining, and cold—not good conditions for spotting a tent site. Very late in the evening, about 12:30 AM, we were told that the next town had a hotel. Tired and cold, we were certainly looking forward to a dry warm mattress to crash on. After at least 45 minutes of hunting, we found the hotel on the second floor of a dark building and it was full—and it was the only one in town. Dejected, we rode around town for a few minutes and found the police station right in the town-square. There were some officers standing around outside just waiting for some crazy Americans to come by so I gestured that we wanted to sleep on our bikes, in the rain, right there, and they gestured ok.

In a handful of minutes Dennis and I had our bikes on their center stands and we were asleep on our seats with our heads on our tank bags, in full motorcycle gear, in the rain, with gloves and helmets securely fastened. It was 1:15 AM and we slept soundly until 4:30 AM. As we were stirring a couple of young entrepreneurs demanded we come across the street for coffee and pizza. We enjoyed the warmth and the hospitality of the morning coffeehouse, combination evening bar, though we were their only patrons at that early hour. The barmaid from the evening before was asleep on the top of the bar—it must have been a good night.

At 5:30 AM we were on our way again, looking for that Russia/Latvia border.—From the Around the World journal

Moscow, Russia

Wednesday, June 9, 2004—*We stopped for coffee at a cafe just 50 kilometers from the border. It turned out that we were 200 kilometers from the border. Just before the border I was stopped for speeding and charged $20 in the way of a bribe. I paid it and moved on. We were concerned about the possible hassle in crossing the border. We had never registered our Russian visas since entering the country. It went very smoothly. One of the young officers gave me a Russian Army arm patch and I gave him my motorcycle card. It took about two hours to go across Russian customs and Latvian customs.*

13

Alps & Dolomites with a Bad Clutch

Thursday, June10, 2004—*We got a hotel in Ludza, Latvia and felt really good to be in a different country for a change.*—From the Around the World journal

Latvia provided me with a feeling of security that I had not experienced in almost a month. My tense body began to relax ever so slowly but it was noticeable. Surely the fatigue that set in during the ride across Siberia contributed to my insecurity. I knew that I was not physically strong then. If any problems developed I could be in "great gobs" of trouble in a hurry. I did not give the insecurity much thought while in Russia because there was nothing I could do to help the situation. We had to get out of the country quickly to satisfy Dennis' 30-day visa—my visa allowed for a stay of 90 days in Russia. Therefore, we did not have the luxury of taking a day or two off for rest and recuperation.

We needed our laundry done again and we were willing to do it ourselves but no luck in Ludza so we rode on. Lunch was in Daugavpils, Latvia, a really neat town. Latvia feels good—like America. The roads are good, the country is clean, and the towns have plenty of amenities. We had begun to relax after having put Russia behind us. Russia felt like a come-and-go concentration camp to me. Dennis said Russia felt like the remnants of a police state. Once again, we were seeing family farms and high-end cars such as the BMW and Mercedes.

In Daugavpils, we decided to look harder for a laundry service. We were directed to a large commercial laundry, and I began the difficult communication process. There were at least nine ladies in the office trying to communicate with me. Dennis watched the bikes. I was trying to make them understand that we were riding motorcycles around the world, and we each had two bags of really dirty laundry and we needed it done quickly so we could continue our journey. After a half-hour I realized I was getting nowhere and someone remembered that there was a young lady upstairs that could speak English. Once we got her involved the laundry started flying in minutes. We had our laundry back in four hours and everything looked good as new again. We were excited—we looked presentable again and probably would not get that dirty again since there would likely be no more dirt roads.

Since it was late in the afternoon, and we were really getting comfortable with Daugavpils, we got a room to spend the night. Actually, we got a palace compared to what we had been used to. It was only $35 per night each but it was very nice—what a treat, clean clothes, a hot shower, and clean sheets. In our spare time we even did a fair job of washing our bikes by hand at a service station.

We left Daugavpils at 6:30 AM the next morning and we were crossing into Lithuania within 15 minutes. Shortly after lunch we stopped in Kalavaris, Lithuania and asked a lady for directions to a moneychanger. We were parked in a parking lot close to her home and I was power napping on Lucille while Dennis was off getting money changed. The lady came over and asked for Dennis and me to join her and her father for tea. I said, "I would talk to Dennis but we were on a tight schedule". As soon as Dennis arrived back at the bikes the lady and her father came running. They would not take no for an answer. We joined them for tea on the gazebo and they brought out coffee, tea, juice, bananas, apples, bread, cheese, nuts, and cookies. What wonderful hospitality they showed us; it was a real delight to meet them. She was a schoolteacher and he was a retired pianist. He gave me a picture of Jesus, and I gave him one of my motorcycle cards. It was a short visit but we all made an impression on each other. I'm really glad that they demanded we stop for a few minutes and interact with them. I really enjoyed their company.

We hit the road toward Warsaw, Poland to put our bikes in the shop for service. After getting gas in Tomza, Poland, Dennis wanted to get some money changed. He bailed out of the last money change due to a long line. It was also time to start thinking of a campsite since it was almost 7 PM. Northeast Poland has beautiful small farms on rolling hills. They were growing numerous types of crops. The ride was good since the roads are well maintained, they are tree lined, and there are plenty of curves.

A gentleman named John, age 50, approached to visit with me while Dennis was at the bank. Pretty quick, I was gesturing for information on where we could camp. He understood my question and he gestured to wait 5 minutes while he fed his guard dogs at his construction company equipment yard. By the tone of their growl I would think his equipment was safe.

Tomza, Poland—John in Back, English Speaking Cousin is Waving, Youngsters Holding Packages Were Getting Married the Next Day

John and his family owned a dairy and he let us camp out in his meadow with the bikes right beside us. They invited us in for dinner and awkward communication and pleaded with us to stay one more day so we could go to their son's wedding. We had to beg off of that due to our tight schedule and lack of proper attire. There were three generations of family living there, with John in the middle generation. We met them all. They fed us breakfast the next morning, and we said our reluctant good-byes. I discovered that people are nice all over the world.

We were gunning for Warsaw on Saturday June 12, 2004 to try and catch the BMW service department before they shut down for the weekend. We got there about 10:00 AM and the motorcycle service department, in the combination BMW Auto/Motorcycle dealership, was closed. That really bummed us out since we were looking forward to getting some needed repairs. We did buy some bulbs to replace our damaged turn signals. We would then have to wait to get the rest of the work done in Munich.

After lunch at McDonalds next door, and an hour of browsing the auto dealership, we were off to Prague, Czech Republic. There was heavy rain to ride through for over an hour. Due to the fatigue of long days and short nights, we were having trouble staying in the saddle.

Since we could not find an isolated spot in the country to camp we opted for a hotel room at Wroclaw, Poland. The cost was $25.50 each for a room with two beds. A shower and a real bed are always a welcome sight after a hard stressful day in the saddle.

On June 13, 2004 we were in Prague and it was my 61st birthday. I wished at the time that my whole family were there to celebrate my world motorcycle adventure and the achievement of my lifelong dream. Dennis and I had a splendid lunch of spaghetti Bolognese at a fine restaurant. It was Sunday and we were the only patrons in the restaurant, but we were a great audience for the entertaining piano player. I was too tired to care. Had I been more refreshed, I would have been depressed that day. Prague is very interesting and a historic city full of romance. My partner in life was a half world away.

The ride through western Poland and eastern Czech Republic was just beautiful, and it really added some greatly needed joy to many moments of the day. Those moments make the trip worth it!

Timing the ride into Munich, a large city, on Monday morning, meant that we should get within 70 miles on Sunday evening, which is just what we did. We found an attractive Bed & Breakfast, Aldersbacher Hof, and the cost was $25 each for a room with 2 beds. The B&B, the room, the little town, and the setting were quite nice but all I got out of it was a quick memory and two pictures. We were still too tired to enjoy and take advantage of our surroundings. I often wondered how many days of straight riding I could take before extreme fatigue set in—I found out on this trip. It was an unusual trip since the Amur in Siberia sapped all my energy. I never recovered until several days after returning home—I tested my endurance. Generally, on my road trips, I don't even have one day like the Amur, let alone eight in a row.

Monday, June 14, 2004—We left the Aldersbacher Hof on time at 5:45 AM and pointed the bikes toward Munich. There was a great deal of trouble finding the BMW Motorcycle dealership due to heavy traffic both coming into the city and within the city. We lacked a good map and we had poorly explained directions. I was a poor leader through crowded, high speed, but beautiful Munich. We found the dealership at 9:30 AM and the service manager took us to the head of the line for writing the service order. They could not have been more accommodating to us poor old worn out Americans.

During the day we were able to have another pleasant spaghetti dinner at a sidewalk cafe nearby and we had plenty of time to explore all the clothing and accessories at the dealership.

I got my headlight fixed which was about to fall off the bike, the fuel overflow flooding problem was repaired, they replaced my rear brake pads, and changed the engine, transmission and final drive oils along with the oil filter. They gave "Lucille" her first bath since Tacoma, Washington and she was fixing to show off.

Dennis' bike had a few more problems than my bike. He got new panniers, a repaired rear brake, new oil and seals in the front forks, a new turn signal, all the oil compartments changed and the wash job. He also opted for a new BMW helmet. I was envious since my relatively new Shoei helmet looked pretty bad with all the duct tape covering the orifices that were letting in too much cold air. We rode for two hours, after paying our large accounts off at the dealership about 5 PM, and then we got a room for the night. We are now 2/3 done with the world tour at this point; we've used 7 currencies, been through 7 countries, changed time zones 10 times while overseas, and ridden 10,000 difficult miles since leaving home 30 days ago.—From the Around the World journal

Tuesday June 15, 2004—We were on the road bright and early this morning and we stopped soon, in Traunstein, Germany, for pastry and coffee. We've been riding very nice, twisty, hilly, roads this morning—more paradise. The Alps Mountains are in view in front of us! Oohrah! "We've ridden through the freezing rain, snow, and black ice of Wyoming; the heavy traffic of Vladivostok, Russia; we dealt with the thugs of Birobidzan, Russia; we fought the jagged rock, sand, mud, hill climbs, and river crossings of 2,000 kilometers in Siberia; and the insane drivers of Moscow; all for a few awesome hours of riding in the magnificent mountains called the Alps. We have arrived! Southeast Germany and Austria are motorcycle paradises with the curvy, tree-lined, hilly roads, and we were fortunate to enjoy perfect temperatures. We just fin-ished dining on sardines, peanut butter, and crackers from the convenience of our panniers in sunny Innsbrook, Austria. This is really living!

From here we are heading toward the Dolomite Mountains of Italy, and we'll look for a campground or an isolated spot in the forest.

It is hard to stay on our route and maintain our direction since the signs keep pointing us toward towns rather than referring to highways. I must have stopped 15 times this morning to verify our direction or to backtrack to the true course (I have not been able to replace my GPS yet).

Lucille is performing real well in this altitude, temperature, and humidity. In an hour I will make my first call to start the process of shipping Lucille from somewhere in Western Europe to somewhere in North America—I'll probably ship about the 26th or 27th. (Note: that plan got altered due to clutch problems taking all my atten-tion).

The Dolomite Mountains of Italy, some of the most beautiful mountains in the world, had many stretches of road construction when we went through including long delays and one lane traffic. Wouldn't you know this is where my clutch problems would develop again? The clutch acted the same three weeks and 8,000 miles ago in Siberia but then the problem disappeared. Now it has reared its ugly head again. I'm shifting without a clutch in the upper gears. In first gear, I have to pump up the pres-sure with several squeezes of the clutch lever, as I'm coming to a stop, to have the nec-essary pressure to disengage the clutch. At least I can still keep moving ahead through the trip but I'm concerned about the inconvenience and safety of navigating these mountain roads without a properly performing clutch. And why did the problem sud-denly resurface? Will it get worse? I don't dare stop and take a picture of this magnifi-cent beauty surrounding me—it's just too awkward and unsafe to stop with a faulty clutch.

We stayed last night in our first commercial campground overseas, just two miles east of Dobbicio, Italy in the mountains; we've never seen a commercial campground until now. The stay at the Olympia Campground was a real joy and comforting—we could have enjoyed a longer stay here. We had the best toilets and hot showers in the world; it doesn't take much to turn me on anymore. There were several other bikers there to talk with and the sight of the surroundings produced the warmest thoughts and feelings—one of the rewards of motorcycling. Before retiring to the tent, I checked the clutch fluid reservoir and I needed to add very little—a lack of fluid was not the problem. I also removed my air cleaner element and knocked the bulk of the residue off that accumulated on the dirt roads of Russia. I should have had the dealership in Munich clean it for me correctly—now I didn't have the necessary equipment to do it right.—From the Around the World journal

We continued on with our Western Europe adventure and stopped at Cortina d' Ampezzo, Italy for coffee. It's difficult for me to drink like the Italians. They would come in and get a jigger full of espresso, gulp it down in one or two swallows, and leave. I'm accustomed to sitting with a large cup of coffee and drinking it slowly, maybe with some conversation—then I might get a refill, but that's not going to happen for me in Europe. Cortina d' Ampezzo has to be one of the most majestic cities in the world—the scenery is absolutely beautiful. I could not get a picture of it when I was high up in the surrounding mountains because of the narrow roads, no shoulders, and the clutch acting up. I'll have to go back someday, for sure, and get a picture.

Lucille's clutch pump went clear out! I had to begin starting and stopping Lucille with the clutch engaged and I was quite busy in the Dolomite Mountains since I was often in the wrong gear for the twisty, hilly roads including numerous hair-pin curves. That created three major problems 1. it was more difficult and unsafe to ride this way, 2. I was more reluctant to stop, and 3. to the public, I looked like someone that just got on a motorcycle that morning for the first time and I would surely kill myself soon.

Starting off from a stop consisted of first gear jumps with a dead engine. I would turn the ignition on while in first gear, hit the starter button and the bike would begin a series of sudden lurches forward. Pretty soon the engine would fire on compression and ignition. Then I could shift to the upper gears by putting pressure on the shift lever and suddenly closing the throttle to release pressure in the transmission. Coming to a complete stop was a matter of shifting down as I approached the stop and I would plan ahead to be in first gear at the stopping point. As I applied both brakes, and held them while closing the throttle, the bike would come to a halt and the engine would die against the clutch engagement. Of course, this procedure looked real cool to the public also, since there were several lurches coming to the stop and I was then sitting there with a dead engine. Taking off again removed all doubt of what they had just seen. I didn't need this challenge but I was thankful that it was occurring in a developed country—one that could easily help me get a repair. And at least Lucille was still able to keep moving ahead.

Lucille Gets a New Clutch Pump at Tag Moto, Bergamo, Italy—We were
Treated Like Aristocrats

Tenting BMW Style—Tag Moto

It was decision time. I would have to get my clutch fixed somewhere along our path and the proposed route included no major cities for 1,500 miles, if not more. The proposed route would take us west from the Dolomites through Switzerland, then south through France and into Spain. I proposed to Dennis that we go south from the Dolomites toward Milan, Italy a major city, get the clutch fixed, and then angle back up north to pick up the route again in Switzerland. He agreed and we were soon locked on for Milan—about 300 miles away.

Roughly 30 miles from Milan, and on the Autobahn, I pulled into one of the auto centers for gas and information. That proved to be a real challenge. I needed to find an English speaking person, that knew the area or how to use the yellow pages in the phonebook, and would help me find directions to a BMW Motorcycle shop. The center had services on both sides of the six-lane highway and they were connected with an overhead, enclosed crosswalk. I was working both sides of the highway, asking anyone that looked suspect, if they spoke English. I had a lot of strikeouts and I was getting discouraged. Ah-hah, I spotted a well-dressed motorcyclist in the restaurant with his wife and he spoke English! Oohrah! I told him I needed to find a BMW motorcycle dealership. He said, "come on out to the bike and we'll look it up". He also was riding a BMW and he had one of the new GPS's that would tell you anything you might need to know. He put in a request for the nearest dealership and the little miracle GPS showed us on a map where it was located from us—just 4 miles away. It gave us written directions on the screen on how to navigate to it from where we were located, it showed us on the map where it was relative to our position, it told us the name of the dealership, the address, and the phone number. That information was a lifeboat for someone like me, new to the area, in a foreign country, speaking a foreign language, and on a motorcycle with no clutch.

We found the dealership, Tag-Moto in Bergamo, Italy, without too much difficulty. I walked into the shop and quickly discovered that no one spoke English. I motioned for them to follow me and I showed the service manager, and the crowd of mechanics, the limp clutch lever with no hydraulic pressure. The service manager pointed to an area clear down in the innards of Lucille and gestured broken. It would take two days to get the clutch pump and get it installed. The first thought I had was, "this will really slow us down". The second thought I had was "hallelujah!" I could really use a two-day break and Dennis was not objecting either.

With Lucille in the BMW clutch hospital Dennis and I would have two days to get some housekeeping items accomplished. The guys at the dealership allowed us to pitch our tents out on the front lawn. There was a convenient grocery store and espresso shop just across the highway. We had an outdoor sink in the back of the dealership where we could clean up some and brush our teeth. The dealership had a tall fence around the perimeter and Dennis and I were in charge of locking the gate at night when we were done coming and going. Tag Moto loaned me a new F650 BMW to get around the city.

The first trip we took from the dealership was following a local that was to guide us to the old historical part of Bergamo where we could find some more spaghetti. It might seem that all we ate was spaghetti—which wasn't true—sometimes we looked for pasta. Well, the local motorcyclist took off like a jackrabbit. I suppose he wanted to impress the two Americans, and he sure did. I was on a new unfamiliar bike and I didn't even know where all the controls were located, such as the turn signals. We were going 60 to 70mph through town, breaking every driving law that you could conceive, and I felt fortunate to have survived. No one was killed and we were soon parked for a leisure lunch. In defense of the local, I quickly discovered that all bikers drive like that in Italy.

Historical Bergamo is wonderful with the narrow streets, old buildings, courtyards, Vespa and Paggio scooters everywhere, and many restaurants to satisfy our cravings. We were there on an average day in June and it was quite the festival.

When the general manager of the dealership, Ezio Righetti, returned and introduced himself to us in Italian; he conveyed that he wanted to take us to a Wine and Cheese Party. We found out that the party was just for us and they spared no cost. I don't drink and Dennis drinks very little but it was a good time for the Italians and the Americans to try to communicate in two languages. The next morning Ezio picked us up at the dealership and took us to breakfast.

It was time to make the call for shipping Lucille across the Atlantic to North America. I called Motorcycle Express in New York and they fixed me up with a flight from Paris to Montreal. They told me I would need to have Lucille at the customs center of Charles DeGaule Airport three days in advance of the flight for quarantine. No problem, I would just enjoy the sights of Paris while I waited for my flight. Motorcycle Express faxed me a contract, I signed it, faxed it back to them, and we had a date to fly Lucille to Canada on June 30. I would fly the same day on a passenger airship. Motorcycle Express needed to mail me some documents for the shipment but I was on the move. I knew I would be up north in a few days so I located and phoned a BMW dealership in Paris and the service manager agreed to receive the documents and keep them in a safe place until I could pick them up. That was agreeable to Motorcycle Express so everything was a "go" on shipping Lucille. Dennis, being retired, decided that he would stay in

Europe a little longer and he would fly out of London. Therefore, we would split up down the road, somewhere in Spain.

Well, the Italians are the greatest people in the world. Tag Moto, Bergamo, fixed the clutch problem and fixed another major problem with the paralever swing arm that was discovered. They would not take a dime for the repair. It had to be around a $600 gift. Tag Moto was added to the list of sponsors for the trip. Dennis bought a new BMW helmet in Germany and he loved it so much that I got one at Tag Moto. They would not let me pay retail for the helmet, only wholesale, and it is a fabulous helmet. We were treated like celebrities all the time we were in Bergamo and we hated to leave—it was one of the most enjoyable parts of the trip.

14

Separated in the Pyrenees Mountains

With two extra days in Italy, I was beginning to think about getting back home to the comforts of my wife, the office, and the dog. It seemed like I had been gone a couple of years but the second leg of the trip from Vladivostok back to Colby was only 52 days. The riding on the highways was less demanding in Europe. I could begin to relax in the saddle and, at times, begin to think of life back in Kansas again. I knew that someday, the trip of a lifetime would be over—that saddened me.

Back in the saddle again, we were heading northwest to pick up the planned route again in Switzerland—in the Alps. Aprica, Italy on Highway 39 was absolutely spectacular. The location of the sun prevented me from getting the picture I wanted as we went over Aprica Pass, which is a must ride for motorcyclists.

We spent that first night, after resuming travel, in a quaint little Bed & Breakfast in Tirano, Italy very close to the Switzerland border. The cost of the room was 50 Euro or $60—ah, a shower again.

Lucille was performing very fine with a new clutch pump. The vibration in the rear that I had been concerned about seemed to be gone also.

Saturday June 19, 2004—We stopped in St Moritz, Switzerland for coffee ($13.00). St Moritz is a ritzy town, and usually I like such a town, but this one didn't feel that good. Generally, I know if I like a town within a few minutes of arriving.

We went over Bernina Pass in Switzerland and the scenery was outstanding. After that we went over Albula Pass which was a very narrow paved road, well above tree line, with plenty of snow off the road. We were meeting lots of motorcycles today; we were in motorcycle paradise. Speaking of paradise, we went over Andermat pass which was fabulous. It was a very high mountain, narrow roads, sheer cliffs for hundreds of feet, plenty of hairpin curves and switchbacks. At times, one can look over the cliff and see all the crazy roads below. Each pass seems to get better then the last one. Still, we were riding with lots of motorcycles. The Alps are great, but I was disappointed in the prices and the people of Switzerland. I'm not being real fair to the country though since, it is small, we went through pretty fast, did not see the major cities, and we did not have a lot of interaction with the people.

We camped just north of Chamoix, France in a commercial campground for 7.5 Euro each. The night was dreary, rainy, and cool—perfect conditions for sleeping in a tent. The campground gave me my first introduction to the open-air toilet for men where women could walk right by. I must say, I was uncomfortable and not accustomed to such an experience.—From the Around the World journal

Rain was coming down when we broke camp the next morning but a little rain is no problem for a couple of drifters like Dennis and I. Once we got the bikes loaded we only had to go a couple of miles and we were in town for a hot breakfast and plenty of espresso. The restaurant was very busy and the people did not seem like they wanted to interact with us. That was disappointing to me. Maybe they were not interested in me—but I was interested in them. Back on the bikes and riding in the rain, the scene didn't change until 11 AM when it was time to stop at McDonalds for coffee.

St Gervais, France reminds me of vibrant Aspen, Colorado, the ski town. Note, towns I really liked on the trip, or found very interesting, and would go back to are: Vladivostok, Russia, Prague, Czech Republic, Cortina d` Ampezzo, Italy, Bergamo, Italy, and St Gervais, France.

We rode from Grenoble, France to Gap in the Alps then on to Montpellier before getting a campsite. The ride that afternoon was filled with spectacular views and roads, as expected. I tend to run out of adjectives to describe the mountainous scenery that we rode through. As motorcyclists, we are always looking for spectacular, magnificent, awesome, and outstanding areas of paradise filled with hills and curves. We had just ridden the roads of that kind of countryside for several hundred miles.

Monday June 21, 2004—We rode down to Parpignan, France, a coastal town just above Barcelona, Spain. Parpignan was the turning point for us to head west into the Pyrenees Mountains. We decided to make this an administrative day after riding just 150 miles.

There was a lot of time spent in boxing up items that we wanted to send home via the postal system. Finding a box, finding the post office, and dealing with the front counter person that did not speak our language were all hurdles for that project. It turned out that sending items home from France was a mistake since it was very expensive. It cost us $120 dollars to send a medium size box to the United States and *we beat the packages home. Dennis found a place to do our laundry in the downtown area while I watched the bikes and we had a lunch from our panniers. A fast food restaurant was convenient for us all afternoon and we must have gone in there 4 times for snacks and coffee.*

This trip was more than I bargained for, especially the dangers of Russia, the length of the trip in weeks, and the distance from home. It was good that Dennis decided to join me on the trip; it would have been a real challenge all alone. I'm certainly not accustomed to spending that much continuous time with one person and I crave solitude sometimes but having Dennis along was very comforting. Occasionally, we were irritable, mostly me, but generally, we got along fine.

Argeles, France, along the Mediterranean coast, was the camping spot for the night.—From the Around the World journal

Breaking camp was easy the next morning. The weather had changed and it was warm and clammy with plenty of airborne insects to buzz us.

I had looked forward to the Pyrenees Mountains but after a few days in the Alps, the Pyrenees seemed like foothills. That was just my impression, sorry Spain and France. The ride on Tuesday June 22 was good though. The scenery and roads were nice and the weather was really cooperating. The road took us through the tiny country of Andorra; I was leading Dennis and following a local on a Vespa scooter. I was impressed with the agility and speed of the Vespa scooter and the skill of the rider. I immediately fell in behind him just to have something to do. He was weaving in and out of the city traffic at high speed, and I was right behind him. We were hitting the lights and having a great time. I was just busy enough navigating traffic that I failed to keep an eye on Dennis. On the other edge of town the traffic lightened up and I looked back—but no Dennis. He probably missed a light or two and fell behind so I stopped along side of the road to wait. There was a sporting goods store right next to my bike so I went inside to check it out knowing, that if Dennis went by, he would see my bike and pull over. I was watching the road from inside the store and "there goes Dennis—he's within three feet of Lucille and didn't see her—he just kept going". It would take me a minute or two to suit up again and by that time Dennis was down the road at least a mile or two. A few miles down the road was the Andorra/Spain border. I waited there for awhile, hoping he would show up, and then I went through the checkpoint, had my bags checked for drugs, and continued on down the road. Soon I was on top of the world again clear up in the top of the Pyrenees Mountains. I pulled over on that sunny day and began to count my blessings. I was so lucky to be in Spain, up in the mountains, on a motorcycle, healthy and happy. The birds were chirping, the flies were passing by, and there was an occasional white butterfly to entertain me. It didn't get any better than that day. The cars were passing by at about one per minute.

I believed that God had directed each part of the world tour and he would direct this situation too. I concluded that I would just continue on through the Pyrenees Mountains and turn north toward Paris on the weekend to get Lucille ready for her flight.

The newly acquired solitude was not disappointing to me, but I was concerned about how Dennis was getting along. On the other hand, I had all the confidence in the world that Dennis was a capable rider and navigator and he would be just fine. Traveling across this part of Spain was not much different than going through Colorado or Utah. Dennis does that all the time.

The road led me to a small village down low in the Pyrenees. It was toward the end of the day so I rented a tent site at a nearby campground—the town was Sore, Spain. I just got my tent erected when, low and behold, there was Dennis pulling in to camp. It truly is a small world. After dinner I watched the young-sters paddle their kayaks through a particularly disturbed section of the river. The kayakers would paddle up the quiet sides of the river and then into the greater velocity section running back down. That produced a ride with great joy and thrill only to repeat the event over and over. Those were not average kayakers; in fact, they were having international competitions there during the day. We don't see a lot of kayakers on the plains of western Kansas so it was interesting to see the skill that those youngsters had developed.

The fuel consumption on Lucille in the Pyrenees was 39.07 mpg; I usually do 10 to 15% better than that back home in the Rockies. The Pyrenees are beautiful in their own way; the people, the weather, the roads, and the scenery were just great. When passing through the tunnels, it was very cold.—From the Around the World journal

It was time for Dennis and me to split up. I had just 2 days to get up to Paris and he wanted to keep on going west. The coffeehouse in Jaca, Spain seemed like a good place to take a break and say our good-byes. Another motorcyclist saw our bikes and stopped to join us for coffee. He asked just enough questions about our travels that we were able to brag about our world tour for at least a half-hour. After coffee, Dennis and I shook hands and agreed that it had been quite a trip. "I'll see you back in the states", were the parting words. The rest of that afternoon I was quite melancholy, knowing what Dennis and I had been through. He was my caretaker for the last 45 days, and I his. Now I was on my own in a foreign country with a foreign language, and all the decisions were mine again—good or bad.

The Alps of Switzerland are Magnificent

I spent the first night on my own at Pau, France. It is a large community and it felt good to be in Pau, a stranger to everyone, and in periods of total solitude.

Thursday June 24, 2004—*Reveille came early as usual, 5:30 AM. Loaded, and on the highway, the first stop was Arcachon, France on the Gulf of Gascogne which is tied in with the Atlantic Ocean. I came through Bordeaux, France this morning; of course it has many growing grapes to eventually sooth some pallets or souse some winos. Corn was also growing in the fields this morning and irrigated fields are becoming common in the landscape.*

Dennis and I are now traveling solo and in different directions. On this overseas leg of the trip, we rode 34 days together and 10,630 miles. For the entire trip, I have covered 12,829 miles to date.

Lucille is running very strong today. Sometimes a motorcycle will really surprise you with extra performance. When the temperature, humidity, and altitude are just right and overcast or darkness helps—she'll put a new smile on your face—today is the day! Lucille is my friend—I must take care of my friend.

Arachon is a beautiful coastal resort area in France about 350 miles south of Paris, which is my destination. There, I prepare to fly to America.

The only thing I will have left for a full "Round the World"(RTW) motorcycle trip is the eastern half of the United States which I have done many times, so I guess I could say I've completed it now—but I won't!

I'll get a few miles closer to Paris today and look for a campsite. "I better get home, all of my Raymond James Financial pens are running out of ink."—From the Around the World journal

Friday June 25, 2004—*Some firsts happened to me this morning. I shaved for the first time since leaving home May 15. I'm just not a beard person. I don't like it, it's not a full beard, it's inconvenient, and the Marines would be ashamed of me, so I'm getting rid of it. I also held up an ATM for the first time in my life—it surely is easier than holding up liquor stores and no one is chasing after me. It's too easy to get Euros out of a little box. As fast as it is, it must be illegal—my Raymond James Debit Account has just been attacked!*

In the morning, the weather was quite cold but then it climbed to 90 degrees by mid day. The highway up to Tours, France was two lanes but this afternoon I'll get on the Autobahn and pay the toll for better speed into Paris. I'll torment the autobahn drivers by only running 95 to 100 mph.

Dennis was right—these tires, Metzler Tourance, with 7,500 miles on them that we installed in Siberia, should last us until we get home. I'm not used to that much performance out of my tires but on the trip, our average speed was much less than our normal 80 to 90 mph. Speed, heat, and improper inflation wear out tires very fast.

Top of the Pyrenees Mountains—Flies, Birds, Butterflies, and Solitude

Lucille will have to be impeccably cleaned before the customs and airlines will accept her for transport. I'll have to work on her for hours this weekend since she's still carrying Siberian mud.

An interesting thing happened two days ago. I was riding way down in a cavernous road beside a river and between two shear cliffs, really enjoying the awesome ride, when I came to a herd of 300 to 400 mountain sheep being herded down the highway by the shepherds. With no shoulders to go to, I just had to stop and let all the rascals go by. Lucille still has French wool all over her. I'm just glad I was traveling against the herd, and not with the herd, or I would still be in the flock somewhere.—From the Around the World journal

15

Prostitutes, Roundabouts &
Charles de Gaulle

BMW Distribution Bobillot was not difficult to find; they gave me good directions and I stopped just once to ask for help. It was of course on Rue Bobillot just northeast of Pl. de Rungis, just south of R de la Colonie which is one way and straight west of Hopital Des Peuplers—yea sure. I hoped that Lucille's shipping papers were inside the dealership.

Paris is a fast paced city. There are motorcycles and scooters everywhere and they know how to ride! I thought I was a good rider but the French put me to shame. One thing they love doing is splitting lanes. That is where they pass vehicles that are side by side and the motorcycle goes up the middle in the 3 to 4 feet the other vehicles are not using. Years ago I did some of that out in California so I had to give it another try. It didn't take me long to realize I'm older, Lucille is larger than the motorcycles they were riding, and I wasn't quite ready to die—at least those are the excuses I gave myself for backing off.

At the dealership the papers were in order and the service manager had them in safekeeping. I bought a BMW T-shirt from them and soon I was on my way to a campground with directions they supplied. The only campground in Paris is the Camping du Bois de Boulogne. The campground on the west side of Paris is next to the Seine River and a part of the large park Bois de Boulogne. It is clean, nice, affordable and very well used by RVs and tenters. While in the campground, I could have Lucille right next to the tent for safekeeping. Plus, it was easy to come and go.

On my way to the campground I traversed the massive Bois de Boulogne Park which was a treat in itself. One thing a Kansan traveling in Paris must be careful of is staring too long at the prostitutes along the edges of the park. With all the traffic it could be hazardous to your health. The prostitutes line the forest in the sultriest pose they can muster. Each girl has a path behind her that leads into the forest. The patron would likely follow her down the path and back into the forest. I suppose some of the patrons lived through it but it sure appeared like a set up for failure to me. Tijuana, Mexico didn't look that scary when some of us Marines went down there in '64' for a little R&R.

Paris has many roundabouts for traffic control and they work very well. Some of the roundabouts would be 7 or 8 lanes wide with traffic moving as fast sideways as forward as they jockey for position. The roundabouts might be almost empty one minute, and just seconds later, after several lights changed down the street, they could be clear full, running 40 mph. I did not see any accidents while I was in Paris. Their traffic control must work very efficiently.

One day, while on foot after giving up Lucille, I wanted to get from Port Maillot, where the bus had let me off, to the retail section across the roundabout. There is an underground walkway system to get pedestrians to the other side safely. I was at street level looking across the 8-lane roundabout that was empty and I thought that would be a shortcut. It seemed odd to me that no other pedestrians had figured out that the shortest route across the roundabout was on ground level and not in the underground walkway. I remember what the teacher said in kindergarten, "Look both ways". I did, so I started running across. I grossly miscalculated the distance and time enroute while crossing 8 lanes of street on foot. Three or four lanes into the crossing, a "cajillion" cars came screaming at me. The roundabout was clear full and just seconds earlier the cars were not even in sight. I can't describe how I looked and felt as the cars were whizzing by at high speed and brushing my front pockets and my rear pockets at the same time. The angels had been put on high alert for Jim Oliver. I put myself in a very dangerous situation and there was nothing I could do to fix it until the traffic dwindled again. I still wonder how much faster the cars were moving because there was a frightened pedestrian "from Mars" out there in the middle of the traffic. The drivers were probably just having some fun with my destiny. Now I remember that the Kindergarten teacher also said, "Follow the directions".

Saturday June 26, 2004—I'm camping at a Central Park like place in Paris for $16 per night—Camping du Bois de Boulogne. It's cheap compared to Hotels and it is complete with hot showers, toilets, and outdoor sinks for cleaning things. I'm camped beside the restaurant, bar, convenience store and reception area for the campground. It seemed like a real good place to pitch the tent since it was convenient—that was an error in my thinking! There was an important Football (soccer) player that showed up last night so there was no sleep for any of us in the general vicinity between 1:30 and 3:30 AM. Hopefully he is gone tonight. There were several sets of youngsters in their twenties camping close by and those were kids traveling Europe for vacation and *adventure. Most of them had a train pass that allowed them to take the train as often as they wanted for a certain period of time; they also used buses and planes to get around. Traveling on foot, basically, with a backpack, is a cheap thrilling way for them to get around. It seems as though everyone smokes in France and everyone buys a two-foot long loaf of fresh bread daily. I bought one this morning along with some strawberry jam—it was okay and I'll have some for tomorrow.*

I spent the morning cleaning Lucille with a toothbrush to satisfy customs check-in.—From the Around the World journal

Sunday June 27, 2004—*Travis, my oldest son, is 39 today. I moved my tent to a quieter location in the campground. I've met lots of people already and discovered a few things. Europeans get at least a month of "holidays", what we call vacation. They have dreams and some are living their dreams. They are very curious about the United States.*

I met a short man, at the campground, from the United Kingdom. He is traveling by train and camping each night; Darryl is his name and he knows a lot about travel. Darryl is a teacher by trade, 42 years old, and he reminded me of a quote from Mark Twain, "he who still has $10,000 in the bank when he dies is a failure!" Darryl interpreted that to mean, don't leave anything to the kids, and have fun with it all.

It is really a beautiful day here in Paris but it will be hot this afternoon. I like my new tent site; I have plenty of space and the tall trees around me provide plenty of shade. Life is so good if you have plenty of shade.

I'm sure of how I feel about motorcycling at this time. This trip had a negative affect on my sport. It was too rugged, too dangerous, and therefore, too long. (Author's note: I see now that the ruggedness of the trip put me in a stupor and it was just now surfacing, probably, because I had time on my hands and I was beginning to "feel" the trip. I remained in that stupor until sometime after returning home. The feelings just described above subsided and I actually feel quite differently several months later.)

Yesterday, I was riding for a bit beside a young mother negotiating Paris traffic rather aggressively on her Vespa scooter. Her son, sitting on the back, appeared to be about 2 ½ years old and that really bothered me. He was holding on but I don't know how since his little arms would only go to her sides and he was too young to problem solve if they encountered any kind of a problem. I see people doing dangerous things and I can not stop them—just as I have done dangerous things and people could not stop me. It is different though for a 2-½ year old. If he were made aware of the possible pain and discomfort he would experience from an accident he would likely choose not to ride on the back of the Vespa, in Metro traffic, until his arms grew a little longer. He was the cutest little boy that I saw in Paris—I sure hope he makes it to high school.

I've concluded that it is one big pain in the ass to ride a motorcycle around the world. (Here comes the stupor again.) *Dealing with shippers of the bike is difficult, dealing with the language barrier is inconvenient and awkward, dealing with per-ceived and real threats to my safety adds stress, and the stress of a possible accident, day after day, must wear me down. I did not see anything out there in this huge world that I could not live without.* Author's note: What I discovered on the world tour is that the people out there in the world are just like Kansans. They are great, fun loving, caring citizens that would do anything for fellow man if he were in trou-ble. The world definitely is worth seeing—it is wonderful to see <u>all</u> of God's cre-ation. Would I do it again, absolutely! Would I do it differently, sure!

Tomorrow, I have to take Lucille to customs at Charles-de-Gaulle airport at 9:30 AM. I rode to the airport and back tonight just to burn off some gas from the tank so it would only have one gallon in her tomorrow—a customs requirement. I was fret-ting about finding the place but it only took 21 minutes to get there. I feel better now about how to schedule my morning.

I'm having coffee by my tent before I go to bed; it is made with my $5 burner that Darryl sold me. I don't know how I have gone without one so long. Coffee is easy, con-venient and fun—let alone inexpensive. I love you—coffee.

I may have a bit of a hassle with my personal flight ticket. I understand Charles-de-Gaulle Airport had a terminal collapse recently and the counter for Air Canada is on the move—it may be fun finding them.—From the Around the World journal

Monday June 28, 2004—*Sleeping was not any better last night. I fixed a strong cup of coffee about 11PM—what a dumb idea. I hate you—coffee. Also, the crossing alarm for the visually impaired pedestrians sounded off every time the traffic light changed and the roadway was just 30 feet away. I kept asking myself, "how many blind people are crossing to the park at 3 in the morning—this is a campground!"*

I got to Expedia Logistics, the shipping agent at the airport for Lucille, about 9:30 AM. I was done with them, customs, and the airline by 11 AM and it went very smooth. I did have to remove the positive cable on the battery and remove everything from the panniers for shipment. Expedia Logistics dropped me off at the terminal so I could pick up my airline ticket that Molly had purchased for me from her end of the world. Now I have my ticket for a Wednesday flight, Lucille flies tomorrow, Tuesday, and I'm all set, except I'm on foot. It was tough saying goodbye to Lucille. We have been close partners for the last 45 days. I just have to trust that the airline will take good care of her. I will take the bus back to Paris just to see how that works for Wednesday.

I am now calling in to the radio station in Kansas, for my daily update on the world tour, from pay phones since I shipped the satellite phone back to Fort Lauderdale to stop the rental. The pay phone works ok but the satellite phone was more fun.

I walked a lot this afternoon looking for a large bag with wheels to carry all of my things on the airline. I will have to carry-on all of my camping gear including a tent, air mattress, and sleeping bag, along with all my clothing and protective riding gear, my tank bag, and everything that was in my panniers. That will be a challenge to get all that to the airport by myself. I am fretting!

I always learn something from every long distance motorcycle trip I take. This time, I fell in love with the United States of America and specifically, with Kansas. The United States has so much to offer the traveler—magnificence, beauty, safety, cleanliness, no nonsense law enforcement and, like many countries, friendly people. Where one finds an abundance of those traits in the United States is in Kansas. It is difficult to find all of that, in one place, in other parts of the world.

A lady asked me what I thought of Western Europe today. I hope I didn't offend her but I said I was really expecting more. She has never been to the United States, I have seen both, and we have the best country.

I learned that I don't like French pastry that I have heard so much about—they don't use enough sugar to suit me and when they say apple-filled I want to see some chunks of apple in there not just applesauce.

I learned that I really like BMW. Their bikes, clothing, helmets, boots, etc. are all a cut-above. They are typically not cheap, but very well built.

I learned to look forward to camping each night. For $300 a couple could be outfitted with a good tent that will protect you from the elements, two thermarest insulated mattresses, and two sleeping bags. If you like the outdoors the way I do, you will save lots of money, have less hassle than motels, and often times, sleep better.

I learned it is pretty important to have someone in this world that you look forward to seeing and they look forward to seeing you.

I learned that vacations are very important for rejuvenation of the body and mind, and working long hours day after day has to be questioned as to the real underlying purpose—and value.

When I started this trip I could not explain why I needed to take it—and I still cannot explain it to anyone's satisfaction. It just needed to be done as a compliment to the sport that I dearly love. Others would surely think I lost what little mind I ever possessed. The sport of motorcycling to me, if done correctly, is truly safe, comfortable, rewarding, challenging, and fun. I would recommend the sport to anyone but, it is very important, to have an experienced and qualified coach and listen to that coach. The coach will do four things for you:

- *Help you build skill*

- *Accelerate the fun*

- *Help develop your confidence*

- *Improve your chances of success.*

—From the Around the World journal

Tuesday morning was spent sorting through things to prepare for Wednesday's flight to Canada. The afternoon was spent looking for another pull type travel bag to haul things to Canada on the airline. Some Australians, Dan & Joy Mahoney, invited me over to their RV for some dinner and conversation in the evening. It was certainly a joy to sit and chat with the Mahoneys as they are intelligent, well read, and have opinions on many world subjects. I got to bed on time but I had some trouble sleeping that night—probably due to the anxiety of the impending hassles with commercial airline transportation.

Wednesday June 30, 2004—*The alarm went off at 4:50 AM and I was staring at the clock making the noise. It is a good thing I started early. The gear did not want to go into the available bags but with plenty of coaxing it was all in there with many bulges. I had to get to Port Maillot, about 4 miles away, to pick up a bus to the airport. I had planned to get a cab to the Port and the on-duty attendant at the campground convinced me that a cab would be impossible at that hour and would be very expensive. Walking a half-mile to the local bus stop, with bags in tow, was the only option. I sucked it up and made the trek but not without breaking into a sweat and I had an equally demanding walk at Port Maillot to get to the other bus stop. Finally, I am on the one-hour bus ride to the airport. The hassle has begun!*—From the Around the World journal

16

Crossing the Atlantic

The Air Canada organization was very nice and accommodating. With just two hours remaining on the seven and a half-hour flight over the Atlantic, I was busy counting my blessings. God has been so good to me—I surely do not deserve his flood of goodness.

Upon landing I discovered that Lucille's shipment was delayed and she would not be in until the next day, <u>and</u> she would be coming into the other airport, Mirabel. It felt so good to be on North American soil again. The airport shuttle took me to the Holiday Inn close to Mirabel where I spent the night. Let's see, I am only two time zones away from home, the electricity in the wall is correct now instead of the funny stuff, most of the people speak English or French and English, and it just feels normal—what I am used to feeling. After checking in to the hotel and getting settled into my room, it was time for dinner, or it was close enough, 5:30 PM. I could hardly stay awake at dinner. It was almost painful to continue with the meal since I was exhausted. I went directly to my room afterwards where I was asleep in minutes. I stayed asleep for 13 hours—my body was coming down!

Thursday July 1, 2004—*"Good Morning Canada"! I love you Canada. It has been a good stay and, hopefully, it will not be a lot longer until I am heading southwest toward Northwest Kansas.*

Road rage appears to be something we developed in North America. I never saw any sign of it overseas and they all drove more aggressively than us, much more aggressively. Within five minutes of landing on American soil I saw a shuttle bus driver leave his seat to go verbally assault a taxi-cab driver who threw the first verbal assault. I do not understand why we think road rage is necessary, when overseas, they have no sign of it and the Americans are the ones with all the blessings.

At the risk of sounding repetitious, I believe that which had such an impact on the trip, negatively, was Russia. The country offered us no indoor plumbing for about 4 to 5,000 miles and that would be about the breadth of the U.S. The language barrier was a huge problem and I cannot blame that on the Russians—they know how to speak Russian very well. And then there were the aggressive men, bold thieves, the worst overall road system I have witnessed with over 2,000 kilometers of continuous road that was open to the public, but should not have been. There were thousands of miles of depressing living conditions, alcoholism to the extreme, huge quantities of large abandoned industrial facilities, a general lack of respect for fellow man, and apparent contentment of the current conditions. Note: The Russian people deserve our empathy for their struggle. The proletariat did not cause the current conditions—they are the result of the past. Just to set the record straight, I do believe in Russia and I currently have a securities investment in Russia. I would go back someday and I would hope that I could stay longer. Good Luck—Russia!

On the positive side, we met some people in Russia that we would not want to forget. Igor and his staff in Vladivostok, the attorney named Butar in Ulan Ude, and the police chief and his friend that gave me the Russian atlas since we said we needed a map. I cannot forget the two non-English speaking ladies at the church that helped us get settled in the church parking lot for the night. I did not think we were going to be able to communicate with them at all but, after 45 minutes, we were pitching our tents at the church. The ladies even brought us bierocks and lemonade for dinner which we ate on our only bench. One of my favorite interactions were the young and beautiful middle school Russian girls that evening that were mesmerized by the two old crazy Americans. The interaction was short, maybe an hour, but it was humorous and a real joy for all. If the girls knew any English they would not admit to it.

A lifesaver was lumberjack John who helped us get Dennis' bike going again in Shemanosk and his church friend who carried Dennis' leaking fuel tank in the family car to a repair shop. I was indebted to the many police departments that secured our bikes for us overnight while we showered and slept in the local hotel. There were the numerous town people that would wave us down and point us back to the illusive Trans-Siberian Highway, and the people that would see our bewilderment in a town—read our sleeping gesture—and lead us to a hotel. Many people showed genuine interest in our conquest and they were in awe—the interest in us made us feel good. The young army soldier that gave me a Russian Army arm patch as I was leaving the country will be in my memory forever. I will not forget all of the car-jockeys that encouraged us to press on day after day with their salutes and waves through Siberia. Note: You may surmise, correctly, that the major impact on me from the world tour was Russia. The route included the breadth of Russia intentionally since the country intrigued me the most. I got everything I bargained for, and more.

The plane from Paris carrying Lucille was a little late. Of course, I was anxious to get possession of her and get on the road again. July 1 is Canada's holiday, like our 4th of July, so I was delighted that the gentleman working the cargo dock was on the job. He was by himself that day and we had an opportunity to get to know each other and learn about each of our countries. I could see he knew more about mine that I did his. Finally, the plane arrived, they unloaded Lucille's metal crate and there she was, just as good as when I gave her up across the pond. I packed her panniers, put on the tank bag, hooked up the battery cable, put on my riding gear, and I was ready to go through customs. My friend, the cargo agent, knew the ropes so he had me cleared with customs by the time I drove over there and all I had to do was wave to everybody and drive through. I was on the road again heading toward home.

It is now 8:25 PM. I got out of Mirabel airport, got through Montreal after some wrong turns, and made it down the road to Dorian before getting a room about 11 PM.—From the Around the World journal

It got so hot in my motel room that night that I elected to get up and take off at 4 AM. I made it across the United States border at Detroit at 2 PM and the border agent cleared me to go, so I pulled up a couple of car lengths to get out of the way to put on my helmet again. The next border agent over was yelling at me and said I had to keep going. I hollered back in the firmest voice possible, "I will, as soon as I put on my helmet"! If looks could kill, he would have been history—and he knew it. I was not in the mood to take a bunch of BS from some a—h—in my own country. I remember one time I unintentionally did something to offend another driver while on vacation and I heard him yell, "Welcome to California, a—h—". Tempers, aggressiveness, hatred, and road rage are a real concern of mine in America. I believe the addition of cellular phones to the situation will greatly compound the problem. In the 12,000 miles covered overseas, through over a dozen countries, never once did I encounter a rude driver.

The speed signs were showing in MPH again after signs in 13 countries with kilometers per hour—hallelujah! I was beginning to see a Wal-Mart every 30 miles. There were cars with United States license plates everywhere in Michigan. Lucille may have a few battle scars from the trip, but she was running real well, so I was happy.

The trip meter on Lucille read 737 miles that day riding through Canada and the United States. The roads were good, the weather was warm, and the traffic was moderate. The traffic was running 85 mph to 100 mph all day so I just jumped into the flow with Lucille. I rode for 13 ½ hours that Friday, July 2. All of the campgrounds that I tried were full due to 4th of July weekend so I was forced to get a cool room at the Red Roof Inn for $59.00.

Saturday July 3, 2004—*After a 600 mile ride southwest to Columbia, Missouri I met Molly at the Holiday Inn. This was the longest we had been apart during our 25 years of marriage and we did not get to converse that much by telephone or mail either. Molly had driven east 600 miles in her sports car to meet me sooner. What can I say, renewal is ecstasy.* Note: Molly shared later, that she was somewhat disappointed in our reunion. She said I just didn't seem that excited to be home. I've never been able to explain to anyone's satisfaction just what I was like at that time but I sure wasn't the real me. I just call it a stupor. My mind had been on a survival mission for so long that it was just going to take me awhile to relax and know that "it was ok"! Then, I would be off the mission and back to some normalcy.

We had a nice dinner at the Olive Gardens tonight and you know what I had—spaghetti. Back at the hotel, I told Molly that I was going to go down the hall and get me a Diet Pepsi out of the machine. I experienced a strange and uncomfortable sensation thinking that I was kind of lost and I hoped that I could find my way back to the room. I knew I was not very far from the room and I was straight down the hall, but it was kind of confusing for me to navigate back down the hallway. Again, after returning to the United States, I believe I had been bombarded with thoughts, feelings and sensations that seemed unusual to me. After being in the "wild" for two months, and on a wicked pace, I was left with some disorientation in my mind. A motorcyclist that cares about surviving never gets a chance to completely relax while riding the bike and my days in the saddle are always long so I don't get a chance to relax that much off the bike either. I cannot imagine what the astronauts must go through when they come back to earth and need stabilization.—From the Around the World journal

It has been quite a trip. The first leg here in the states, getting Lucille to Tacoma, Washington, and getting back home was eight days. Lucille turned over 50,000 total miles at Columbia, Missouri. My written goal, from five years back, was to circle the globe by motorcycle by age 60. I finished the trip at age 61 and 22 days. Some experiences included:

- The longest day—the first one out of Vladivostok to Birobidzan, 20 hours and plenty of problems including robbery.

- The nicest person for me—Ezio Righetti, General Manager of Tag Moto BMW, Bergamo, Italy

- Worst highway—Trans-Siberian Highway in Siberia, 6000 miles

- Worst section of the worst highway—Amur area of Siberia, 1,300 miles

- Most cherished sleep—in front of the police station, with their permission in Russia—we slept in the saddle of our bikes, in full riding gear, in the rain, for three hours without waking.

- Best mountain range—Dolomite mountains @ Cortina de Ampezzo, Italy

- Most cherished food—Mexican food in, of all places, Perm, Russia—Siberia.

- Second most cherished food—McDonalds @ Moscow

- Biggest surprise—Our extreme fatigue and the number of bad miles of road. We had trained for the trip, were in pretty decent physical condition and it still exhausted us.

- Biggest concern—shipping the bikes by sea but it went very smooth

- Most treacherous traffic—Vladivostok, Russia, it was very fast and very aggressive.

- Greatest moment—meeting Molly at Columbia, Missouri

- Nicest people—Bergamo, Italy

- #1 place to return to—Prague, Czech Republic

- Never want to see—another Russian traffic control checkpoint

- There was too much—Borscht soup, bad roads, potholes, dishonest people, weight on the bikes

- Three things that work well—ATMs, International phone cards, and International Driving Permits

- Food Surprises—There was no peanut butter overseas that I could find, no smoked oysters in the can, and most bottled water in Russia has gas in it. If you ask for coffee they give you espresso, they never serve butter with bread, and Diet Pepsi is Pepsi Light. Every cafe in Russia, at every meal, likes to start off with a big bowl of their beet soup—borscht, and everyone in France buys a new loaf of bread every morning.

• Gas surprise—it was plentiful in Russia but the quality was erratic, sometimes the bike wouldn't even run on the Russian gas, and it would be easy to confuse diesel with gas at the pump in Russia.

• Bike surprises—our GS, on/off road bikes were too heavy as loaded in Russia but they took an exceptional pounding in the Amur with grace, and they did the job. Neither bike ever failed to keep moving forward. The F650 BMW might be a better choice for Siberia though.

• Packing surprises—my Helen-2-Wheels bags worked exceptionally well but my Big Mac tank bag wanted to come off if packed too heavy. My Bill Mayer custom seat worked well but a seam came apart which I duct taped and they fixed it at no charge when I got home, our stock windshields worked well, and our two sets of Metzler tires, on two bikes, worked very well. The Aerostich Darien Pants and Jackets are worth the high price—they really work.

17

Afterword

Within each of us is the power to do things we never dreamed possible, as depicted in the movie, *Facing the Giants*. This power surfaces just as soon as we change our beliefs from "I can't" to "I can". We need to always remember the incredible power of childhood, when everything seemed possible, while fear of failure was still absent from the thought process—we felt invincible. Then, someone came along and started implying that we really could not fly like Super Man. Slowly, in our life, belief is replaced with disbelief and the ability to dream is lost.

I believe there is a cause and effect to everything. If I get a thought, then I must next decide if I want to act on it, or let the thought die. There will be a result on the thought whether I act on it or not. The seed of my around the world adventure was, no doubt, planted in my mind many years ago when I took that great ride down a steep hill in Topeka, Kansas, at age three.

The world motorcycle trip has made me famous locally. Not so much because I did anything so great, but because I was on the radio Monday through Friday giving the public a running account of the ongoing saga. The public loved it, and they were able to take the trip with me from the comforts of their family room, car or office. I called in from some of the most remote areas of the world. A couple of times I was just unable to call in due to a crazy schedule and the public was calling the radio station and asking, "Do you think they are all right"? The radio station, KLOE/KKCI of Goodland, Kansas, was as stunned as I of the interest that the broadcasts generated. I have produced a weekly financial service half-hour broadcast on KLOE for the last five years, so I was not completely foreign to the listening public.

Speaking engagements, especially to women's clubs, were numerous for me after the conclusion of the trip. Women seem to show more interest in adventure than men. Several newspapers did excellent write-ups on the expedition, and I was interviewed on the radio a few times both before and after the trip. Even months later I would have people tell me on the street that they listened to every broadcast while I was circling the globe.

I must say, with the interest that I have developed in motorcycling over the years, it feels very good to have had so many other people following my story on the sport. I'm always interested in promoting motorcycling as a clean, safe, fun, mode of transportation and entertainment.

Circling the globe was surely the trip of a lifetime and a dream come true. I had dreamed, thought, felt, and lived the trip since I was a child and the actual event proved to be everything I knew it would be. I had all the confidence necessary that I could safely ride a motorcycle around the world. I believed that God was ok with the trip. I could visualize the daily struggles and the completion of the trip in my mind. What I did not know was if the tigers would attack or if my partner could make it. Adventure is thrill-filled.

My emotions ran high before and after the trip but not so much during the trip. When on stage, we must have our thinking cap on and not our feeling cap. Before the curtain goes up we may be very emotional and when it goes down we may be weeping. I learned in the U.S. Marine Corp, when facing the enemy there is no room for emotion. On this trip the enemy was the unknown and the barrage of challenges. I could not show emotion before the trip to family or friends for fear they would lose confidence in me. I sure wanted to show emotion though.

As I was preparing for the trip I often asked myself, "What have I asked of my family?" I'm the only avid motorcyclist in my family. Therefore, no one else understands the confidence level that I maintain. They only know the fear emotions and the "what ifs". My stepson Jarrod, a U.S. Marine himself, probably understands me better than anyone. Jarrod understands adventure and he has had professional motorcycle instruction. At one time, he was supposed to join me on the world tour. Unfortunately, that did not work out and I am deeply disappointed that he was not part of the trip of a lifetime.

It is interesting for me to think about how all of this happened. Over the years, Molly winced at some of my motorcycle trips as I was preparing to leave. She asked me not to go many times but always allowed me to make the final decision. She let me be me. I am so thankful for that because I have grown as a result of her allowing me to grow. I want to grow and I want to explore; it is an important part of my makeup.

I asked my family to endure a lot by allowing me to go off into the wild blue yonder with only Dennis to pick me up if I fell down. They have seen me do many things over the years that others might choose not to do, but I have had more fun than most. Those experiences are important to me. I felt an obligation to the family to take care of myself and to get home quickly. I only allowed 60 days for the trip and that is exactly what it took. Looking back, it is obvious that I pushed myself very hard to achieve the goal in a timely fashion. A great deal of the stress came from the clock ticking away every day while I was circling back to the starting point.

My financial advisory practice is a very important part of my life. I have the best clients in the world. I tried to keep them abreast of what was happening, when I would leave, when I would be home, and what they should do if they needed something while I was gone. Calling into the radio station everyday with a brief update allowed me to talk subconsciously to my clients, many of whom listened to every broadcast. The business carried on very well without me while I was gone; I think I should be concerned.

Of all the modes of transportation available to see the world, the best one is the motorcycle. There are no obstructions to your view, you are "in" the scene, and you smell the land and feel the country. There is no better feeling than a ride through the country on a beautiful day.

Our thoughts both negative and positive are powerful forces of energy that can only come from within our own minds. We each get to create our thoughts that are ultimately converted into events. Since our thoughts create reality, we create our own reality. Negative thoughts yield negative reality. The trick is to think positively and to get God's help through prayer. Just as the conscious mind is the source of thought, the subconscious mind is the source of power. The mind will create anything we tell it to create; I do believe that and I admit, it is a challenge to implement, but worth the attempt.

The fear of death follows from the fear of life. A man who lives fully is prepared to die at any time.

—Mark Twain

APPENDIX A

Things to Consider Taking Along

The following is a list of things to "consider" taking along on a long trip. Here's a tip: consider only the absolutely necessary items. Lay them all out. Then put half of the items back on the shelf—seriously. Excessive weight and height on your bike is crucial. Remember that you will likely have to pick up the bike many times in rough conditions and the suspension, tires, and rims do have limits.

Novel (for rain out days)	Motorcycle Ins. Card
Carnet de Passage	Intl. Driver Permit
Mother Wallet	Playing Cards
Business Cards	Passport and Visas
Personal Organizer	Writing Journal
Document Copies	Service Manual CD
Batteries	GPS
Electronic Translator	Motorcycle Title
Motorcycle Registration	Bible
Magnifying Glass	Waterproof Gloves
Deerskin Gloves	Helmet
Extra Face Shield	Electric Vest
Waterproof Jacket	Ski Mask & Goggles
Wind Bloc Jacket	Long Underwear
Light Poncho	Turtleneck Shirts
Matches	Folding Shovel
Grate for Cooking	Transistor Radio

Detergent

Toilet Paper

50' Cord

Can Opener

Whistle

Hatchet

Mess Kit

Emergency Blanket

First Aid Kit

Malaria Pills

Spare Glasses

Itch Creme

Antiseptic Powder

Petroleum Jelly

Towel

Bead Breaker

"Slime"

Tubeless Plugs and Tools

Extra Valve Cores

Extra Engine Oil

Tent w/Rain Fly

Thermal Mattress

WD 40

JB Weld

Grease

Sand Paper

Hacksaw

Spare Bulbs and Fuses

Insect Repellent

Cable Saw

Scouring Sponges

Water Purifier

Hand Sanitizer

Mosquito Head Net

Knife, Spoon & Fork

Dr's Emergency Pills

Sun Bloc

Survival Guide

Tweezers

First Aid Book

Lip Balm

Wash Cloth

Extra Tires

Tire Irons

Air Compressor

Tire Patches

Valve Core Remover

Sleeping Bag

Footprint

Pillow

Electrical Tape

JB Kwik Epoxy

Ball Peen Hammer

Electrical Tester

Loctite

Siphoning Line

Round Metal File	Toothbrush/cleaning
Cable Ties	Stanley Knife
Sharpening Stone	Oil Filter Wrench
Finger Nail Polish	Razor Blades
Duct Tape	Extra Spark Plugs
Magnetic Screw Starter	Tire Gauge
Long Handled Mirror	Needle Nose Pliers
Vise Grips	10 in 1 Knife
Gasket Sealer	Collapsible Bucket
Multi Fuel Stove	Cook Pots
Camera	Extra Passport Photos
Spare Keys	Compass
Maps	Guide Books
Hat	Waterproof Boots
Protective Waterproof Clothing	Lighter Rain Gear
Sunglasses	Swim Suit
Sandals	Satellite Phone
Install New Motorcycle Battery	"Miner's" Light
Prepaid Medical Evacuation Card	Money Belt
Repair Sewing Kit	Flashlight
Bike 2 Bike Communication	

APPENDIX B
Motorcycle Related Web Sites

Alex's BMW Motorcycle & Global Touring Page
http://www.ott.igs.net/~ace

"Riding the Edge" by Dave Barr
www.davebarr.com

BILLMAYERSADDLES, custom motorcycle seats, the Original Mayer Saddle
http://www.billmayersaddles.com

BMW MOA Global Touring
http://www.bmwmoa.org/global

Bureau of Consular Affairs, US Department of State
http://travel.state.gov

Colorado Beemers.com
http://www.coloradobeemers.com

Foliage Central—Bagging the Peaks
http://www.newengland.com/foliage/chart.html

Froggtoggs.com
http://www.froggtoggs.com/index.html

Globebusters.com
http://www.globebusters.com

Globeriders.com
http://globeriders.com

Globetrott Zentrale Bernd Tesch
http://berndtesch.de/English/EIndex.html

Horizons Unlimited—THE Motorcycle Travel site
http://www.horizonsunlimited.com

IBMWR—BMW Motorcycle Mailing List
http://ibmwr.org

Iron Butt Association
http://ironbutt.com

Jesse Luggage Systems
http://jesseluggage.com

Gear Online Catalog Motorcycle Riding Apparel Suite
http://www.aerostich.com/riderwearhouse.store

Lonely Planet Online
http://lonelyplanet.com/

Get Directions
http://www.randmcnally.com/

Milward's Millennium Motorcycle Ride
http://www.millennium-ride.com/

Motorcycle World Challenge
http://motorcycleworldchallenge.com/

BMW Motorcycle Club
http://pikespeakriders.org/

Racer Apparel
http://wearracer.com/

Ride of the Heart, Mariola Cichon going around the world
http://rideoftheheart.com

RiderReportcom Motorcycle reviews, news and features from the editors of Rider, Cruising Rider and Woman Rider.
http://www.riderreport.com

The Return of Jupiter's Travels
http://www.jupitalia.com

Touratech USA
http://touratech-usa.com/

Whitehorse Press Motorcycle Books, Videos, Maps, T-Shirts, Posters, Tools, and Accessories
http://www.whitehorsepress.com/

Wolfman Motorcycle Luggage
http://wolfmanluggage.com/

Cycle Gadgets Accessories
http://www.cyclegadgets.com

BMW Windshields, Fairings
http://www.parabellum.com/

Cee Bailey's Motorcycle Products
http://www.ceebaileys.com

Helen Twowheels Super Packing System
http://www.helen2wheels.com

Marsee Products
http://www.marseeproducts.com

Moto-Charlie.COM
http://www.moto-charlie.com

Professional Audio for Motorsports
http://www.autocomamerica.com

Bikers Without Borders
http://www.bikerswithoutborders.org

Aerostitch Riderwear
http://www.aerostich.com

The Turtle Expedition
http://www.turtleexpedition.com/

24 Hour US Passport and Travel Visa Express Service for United States Passport
Renewals and First Time Applications
http://travisa.com/

U.S.Embassy-Moscow
http://moscow.usembassy.gov/

VirtualTourist.com
http://www.virtualtourist.com

BMW Club of Colorado
http://coloradobeemers.com/

Get your visa to Russia—full Russian visa service.
http://gotorussia.com

GPS Receiver Information, Software, and Hardware
http://gpsinformation.net/

Motorcycle Express
http://motorcycleexpress.com

Search for Flights
http://www.expedia.com/

EBay Motors
http://motors.listings.ebay.com

IBMWR BMW Motorcycle Marketplace
http://www.ibmwr.org/market/

Maritime Cargo Shipping—FESCO Agencies NA
http://www.fesco.com/

Northern Colorado BMW—Ducati Motorcycles
http://www.bmwducati.com/

Motorcycle Safety Foundation
http://msf-usa.org/

Adventure Rider
http://advrider.com/

BMW Motorcycle Models
http://bmbikes.co.uk/bmwmodels.htm

Honda Motorcycles
http://powersports.honda.com/motorcycles/

The Millennium Adventure
http://www.jimrogers.com/

Motorrad Media
http://www.motorradmedia.com/

Yamaha Motor Corporation
http://www.yamaha-motor.com/

Happy Trails Motorcycle Products
http://www.happy-trail.com/

How Does a Motorcycle Work?
http://motorcycles.about.com/cs/beginners/a/howdoesbikework.htm

1Tail Sportbike and Roadracing Accessories
http://www.1tail.com/

Jim Key in Central America
http://goxplor.blogs.com/

Adventurerider.com
http://adventurerider.com/

BMW MOA Beyond Europe
http://www.bmwmoa.org/global/BeyondEurope.htm

Big Dog Adventures
http://bigdogadventures.com/

APPENDIX C

The Ten Commandments of Motorcycling

1. Never ride beyond your skill level

2. Never ride at the level of fatigue

3. Always know your tire condition—tread depth, sidewall condition and pressure

4. Never ride in the other guy's blind spot

5. Always keep someone posted as to your condition and whereabouts

6. Always ride the proper size bike for the trip

7. Don't even get on a bike until you have successfully passed the Motorcycle Safety Foundation—Safe Rider Course

8. Never ride to show off

9. Always ride with the proper equipment

10. Take God along every time

978-0-595-41724-7
0-595-41724-8

Printed in the United States
76583LV00005B/169